RAI
SCITUATE'S SPIRITS

LOCAL STORIES OF PARANORMAL EVENTS

Christine
Yours in 'spirit,'
Kathie Lee
3/15

Kathie Mason Lee and J. Neal Gray

Llumina Press

A portion of the proceeds of each book will benefit The Scituate Food Pantry and The Scituate Historical Society.

Cover photo by J. Neal Gray

Library of Congress Control Number: 2005925801

ISBN: 1-59526-007-2

Printed in the United States of America by Llumina Press

TABLE OF CONTENTS

Acknowledgements:

Most of our contributors have requested anonymity. I think you will see that we have met that obligation. However, we are also obliged to thank them for giving so greatly of their time, energy, hospitality, kindness, and some mighty fine stories! Thank you, Dear Hearts, for all that you gave us and our readers.

I wish to thank my sons: Patrick, Christopher, and Daniel; my daughters-in-law, Mary and Beth; and my grandson, Bob, for their love and support. A special thank you to Chris, who shares a sensitivity and an acceptance of the mystic aspects of life and who will never be far away from my heart. I also thank my father for constantly badgering me with, "Let's get this project done!!! What are you waiting for?" etc. He has always supported me in any endeavor and is always a love of an old goat. Thank you, too, to Martin, whose sublime Irish mysticism has been a guiding force through the last 10 years.

Neal and I have remained friends throughout this project; a tribute to the omnipotence of the human spirit. Actually, working with Neal is a joy and a great source of comfort. Thank you for being a driving force and for your kindness to me!

Kathie

Acknowledgements:

As Kathie has so eloquently expressed; we are grateful to all those who gave us encouragement and caustic comments along the way. And we did drop the ball for quite a while due to major changes, particularly in Kathie's life. The unexpected death of her husband Bob left her with a home to manage and bringing her youngest son through the grief as well. Now that he is off to college, we found ourselves thinking it was time to wrap up the book. Many hours went into the book these past few weeks.

My daughter Mimi and her husband Joe were always most supportive and even helped us find new places to investigate. I can't go far without thanking my old friend Robert Fraser; long-time resident of Cohasset and a writer himself. He supplied much information about unseen things in Cohasset, especially about Cohasset's Maritime Museum ghost. Bob was present at the meetings in the museum when footsteps were heard upstairs. He was the one who went up to investigate who was making the noise. Other friends contributed their knowledge of ghosts and as Kathie stated they wanted to remain anonymous. Our sincere thanks go out to you as well.

Working with Kathie has been a marvelous experience. We worked without any animosity towards each other's ideas. It's almost like we are one person, but each with our own little gems to add to the finished jewel. Kathie writes far more fluidly than this writer who sees the words on a page as a picture; not just words and sentences. Thus, if the balance isn't right, I will meander back and forth until I'm satisfied with how it *looks*.

J. Neal Gray

RAISING SCITUATE'S SPIRITS

LOCAL STORIES OF PARANORMAL EVENTS

Neal's Prologue

Introduction

Where do they come from? Who are they? Why don't they leave? Why are some friendly and others not friendly? Why can children see them sometimes and we cannot? Why, why, why?

The tales of the supernatural have fascinated us for hundreds of years. Many people, no, let's say most people will say none of the following story is true. I am making all of this up to make money. If that were true, I could write a more fascinating book; maybe science fiction, a romantic novel, or murder mystery.

Well, let me put it to you very clearly – wait until you experience or see something you can't explain. Then, then you'll know. I know.

The Engineering Firm

My experiences span many years. I guess the first took place in Boston in a very modern building, a very conservative company, in the middle of the day, in a well lit room, with two other witnesses looking on and trying to believe their eyes while I was doing the same thing.

But we're getting ahead of ourselves. Let's look at the very beginning of this event and circumstances that led up to this – my first experience of seeing something I couldn't explain.

I worked for an old long-established Boston engineering firm. They had opened a new modern building of fourteen floors during the years when nuclear power plants were thought to be the future of America's electrical power generating plants. I was a support engineer in the Materials Engineering Section where we tested materials going into these plants to make sure they were of the proper quality to meet the specifications set down by the Nuclear Regulating branch of the US Government. The entire force of our section was highly qualified engineers who had many years of experience in their particular field of expertise.

One such person was Douglas Warner (not his real name). He was a welding engineer. He had one habit that annoyed the rest of us. He had a cigarette going almost every minute of every day. He would come in to work in the morning with his cigarette and his coffee. We would try to upset his routine by shooting elastics at his coffee cup or at his cigarette. On one occasion we did manage to use a big enough elastic to knock his coffee over.

Anyway, at Christmas one year, Doug was going to upstate New York to visit a relative. He had what he thought was a bad cold and a very bad cough. He drove up there with his 13-year-old son.

It was cold and snowing and near Albany, NY. He could drive no further, as he felt very dizzy and pulled into a motel. His son called the relative who drove down, saw his condition, and called an ambulance. Doug's "cold" was pneumonia. Doug didn't make it. He died on Christmas Eve.

Christmas that year came in the middle of the week. Due to the press of business, three of us were asked to work over the weekend after Christmas. We were all in one 20-foot square cubicle, open on two ends. Two desks were on one side and two on the other. Separating each pair of desks was a worktable with an aisle in the middle.

It was about ten o'clock in the morning, everything quite normal, when suddenly, our cubicle got as cold as though we had moved into a refrigerator. Startled, we looked up from our work and looked at each other. Then they looked out one end of our area. I turned to look at what they were looking at – Doug was coming towards us. It was no doubt that it was him even though he was sort of made of smoke. His facial features were clearly discernable. His gait was just the same.

Due to the height of the partition I couldn't tell if he had his coffee and a cigarette until he turned the corner and came into full view. He did not. I was somewhat frightened – no, I was scared out of my wits. I got up on the table to see where he was headed. My co-workers got up and decided to follow him. He turned the corner and headed towards the boss' office. The faster my co-workers walked, the faster he walked. He turned into the boss' office and when they got there he was gone.

They searched the boss' office thoroughly. They came back, sat down, and we looked at each other. We asked ourselves – did we see a ghost? Three people couldn't have fallen asleep and had this dream all at the same time. One of my co-workers was a no-nonsense type of guy. He was *thoroughly* shaken. If you'd asked him before this event if he believed in ghosts, he would have given you an emphatic NO! Now his whole life was changed by Doug's appearance.

Well, we jokingly said to ourselves he'd come back to get his paycheck, but knowing Doug, he came back to tell the boss he had died; pure and simple.

On Monday, our experience became the talk of the entire company. We were questioned constantly about all the details. Some people even hinted we made it all up. Well, we wrote a song about it to the tune of "Temptation":

He came, we were alone,
We should have known,
It was Doug Warner. etc.

The following weekend, it was after New Year's, and we three were again working on overtime.

This time however, we had a secretary typing up some of our reports. We talked a lot early in the morning as to whether Doug would re-appear. At exactly the same time, the instant cold returned and we knew Doug was here again. The difference was, he walked by the secretary before he got to where we were sitting. She let out a SCREAM that could be heard for miles. He disappeared.

My guess is, to materialize, he has to take all the heat (energy) out of the air. That's why it got so cold, so quick. When she screamed, it upset the balance of the air and he could no longer maintain his ability to be visible.

Frank did not come again; at least not in a visible form.

In two weeks, the secretary, a very devout Roman Catholic, quit her job. She said she couldn't work there thinking he might come again. All her religious training had told her the ghosts did not exist. Yet she saw Doug with her own eyes.

And so did we.

Neal's Sprites

A lot of Scituate's unexplained happenings occur only once. They don't repeat themselves on a daily, monthly or yearly basis. Once, and they're done. Why, we don't pretend to know. Maybe the spirit is a long term resident in the house he occupies and is only mildly upset when something occurs to change his/her surroundings.

Other unexplained events happen in one place in the home and although they're not a frequent event, they remind the owners every once in a while. "Hey, remember me?"

This is a compilation of several of those happenings:

The Mann House

The Historical Society in Scituate likes to have tenants live in the houses that belong to the society. It has a double-edged benefit. It brings money into the society's coffers, plus, with someone living in the house there is less chance of robberies or vandalism.

A while back, Percy Mann's historic house in Scituate received a new tenant. As she was undressing the first night, suddenly the door was flung open. Although she could see no one, she instantly grasped the situation and spat out; *"Percy, don't ever come in this room again without knocking!!!"*

It must have been Percy as it has never happened again.

Near St. Mary's Church

A house close to St. Mary's Church in the harbor has a resident spirit *outside*. Where does he/she go in the winter? Don't spirits feel the cold?

Anyway, when the owners are doing the gardening out front near the street, they have the distinct feeling they are not alone. It's as though someone is watching their every move. Also, coolness often felt when a spirit is nearby. They have no idea who the presence is, but are not upset by the presence as it never moves or borrows any tools. Plus, they have a pleasant feeling about the presence. This is fairly common when friendly spirits are nearby. Recently, he was seen wearing a t-shirt and crossing the driveway.

Hatherly Road

A big house on Hatherly Road was recently up-graded and in so doing the new owners enclosed a porch and glassed it in. This necessitated a new front door to the porch. For better insulation in the winter, they left the old front door between the porch and the house in place.

In the center of this old door was one of those door-bells that you twisted the handle it went, "brrrrrring". On the first night with the new door installed, the owner locked the new outside door and, not thinking, also locked the old door.

As he was climbing onto bed he heard "brrrrrring", so he went down stairs wondering how someone could have gotten in through the new door to ring the old bell. No one was there. This was perplexing, but he thought it might have had some-thing hanging on the knob and the weight finally caused the bell to ring. Back upstairs he asked his wife if she had heard it, again wondering if he was the only one to have heard it.

She said that she heard it, too. So he got into bed again and settled down for the night and "BRRRRING," off it went again, this time seeming a little louder. He got his pistol out and went down stairs again. Perhaps someone was inside trying to get out. No one was at the door. He made a thorough search of the house.

Nothing was out of place. He decided to issue a warning and felt foolish talking to "thin air" or someone he couldn't see. He said; "Don't bother me again!"

And it, they, or whoever hasn't rung the bell since.

Barker Road

My friend Frank Handy lives in a house owned for many years by the founder of the Scituate Harbor Yacht Club. The Scituate Yacht Club went broke in 1940 and John Quinlan and others got together and reorganized the club and paid off the old debts of the original club.

Mr, Quinlan was a heavy smoker. Frank and his wife Joan often detect the smell of cigarette smoke in what was Mr. Quinlan's bedroom. They also occasionally get the same thing in the living room even though no one has smoked in the house in many years.

Why only the smell? They never feel the coolness when a spirit is nearby; only the smell.

The Collier House

At the corner of Glades and Gannett Roads there used to be a very early house known as the Collier

House. It was built in the 1700's and the Collier's kept a slave to do the chores. At night, he was fastened by a chain around his ankle to a center bolt in the floor in the attic.

In winter, must have been very cold up there at night. He would pace around the center bolt to stay warm. One night he got hypothermia and the sleepiness that goes with it, lay down to sleep and froze to death. Every cold night afterwards, the owners would hear the sound of the chain being dragged around and around in the attic. It must have been very unnerving.

In the 1960's the house was being restored. During this work, it caught fire one night and burned down. The reason was never found.

The Scituate Harbor Yacht Club

Past Commodore XXX of the yacht club, in his doting years, took a great interest in making sure everything was shipshape at *his* yacht club. Every morning, he would ask one or more of the hired help or other members if everything was OK. He also would reiterate (every day) that whatever improvements had been done to the club were done during his tenure as commodore. He died the year before this episode took place.

That was some time ago. The next summer a nor'easter came up, and it was customary for the club's Steward to check all the boats in the Marina to make sure member's boats were secure.

The Steward was joined by the Marina Chairman and they were making some small talk as they wiggled onto their foul weather gear. It was a struggle putting these clothes on over their already damp clothing. As they worked at it, their conversation trailed off. The Steward felt a person walking behind him and assumed it was the Marina Chairman. He looked up and saw the Marina Chairman halfway out on the walkway. Then, he turned to see who was walking by him and a solid black figure was on his way through the door (it was closed).

Once outside, the figure faded away!

When he discussed this with me, I mentioned our gruff, but friendly old commodore and we *knew* it was him. He'd come back to make sure everything was OK and to check on things because of the impending storm.

First Cliff

A house on First Cliff in Scituate had a fastidious spirit. The people who lived in the house several years ago were surprised to find the downstairs, especially the kitchen and the living room, tidied up each morning. It happened every morning that they owned the house. When they first realized it, they weren't sure what it was. To check and make sure they weren't doing it and forgetting it the next morning, they made lists of where things were when they went to bed. In the morning, of course, everything was straightened out and pristine.

I could use one of those – I wonder if he/she hires out!

Cohasset Central Cemetery

My nephew mentioned that when he was a teenager; he and three others were coming from a party with a few beers and their route led past the Central Graveyard in Cohasset. This graveyard has some raised tombs out front with big iron doors and covered with soil and grass. They plopped themselves on top of one of these with their feet dangling over the front edge. They were just about to open the beers when there was a *LOUD THUMP* from inside the tomb they were sitting on. I believe they set a new record from the graveyard to the center of town that night!

Peg Leg Ghost

Another interesting ghost was in a house on North Main Street area. The owner, somewhere in his travels at sea, lost one of his legs below the knee and had a peg leg. He and his wife slowly drifted apart because she had frequent social tea parties in the afternoon and he would come rolling in from the local pub making irreverent remarks to the assembled ladies. Finally, she had an outside stairway added to the house for him to go up to his room without disturbing the ladies.

After he died he could still be heard clopping around upstairs in his room.

Old Inn and Tavern

There's a well known very early tavern is Scituate that is supposed to have been part of the "underground railway" used to ferry slaves to Canada to escape prosecution. Supposedly a tunnel ran from the tavern to the harbor and evidence of this tunnel was discovered when foundations for houses were built in later years. This tavern has had many unusual happenings.

One story goes that there is a table in the dining room that can't be set up until the guests are standing in front of it. If they make it up any earlier, it is covered with dust and the place mats and napkins in disarray in a few minutes.

An ex-head hostess tells that at the end of the evening when she would bring the night's receipts up to the owner who lived upstairs, she would feel a cool "presence" (as she called it) pass her on the stairs. The "Bride's Room" upstairs is the center of a lot of the activity.

Another hostess will not go in one of the storerooms in the cellar. This room is where the tunnel is supposed to have come into the tavern.

The owner no longer lives upstairs. Maybe the "presence" has won.

Country Way

On Country Way in Scituate very near "Indian House" stands another historic house. This house must have been at one time the home of a seafarer. He apparently was lost at sea, because his widow and baby are still waiting for him. She often appears as a very solid person. Not in smoke or semitransparent as some ghosts do.

My friend's first encounter was the day he moved in. This took place some years ago. After a long day of moving in their belongings, they sat on the floor in the living room for some coffee. Cushions for the sofa were still in boxes. Suddenly, they heard footsteps coming down the stairs and into the room walked this woman with her child in her arms. She parted the lace curtains that actually weren't there and looked out the window for what seemed like a few minutes.

My friend and his wife were taken aback, but did not feel threatened. Actually they felt empathy with her and thought they should ask her if they could help in any way. They had no idea how she got in the house as no one was there all the time they were moving things in. But as they started to speak to her, she faded away!

She returned many times, but usually in the same manner looking out the window. Yet, there was at least two occasions where things were different.

One night my daughter and her husband were babysitting for their mutual friends and they heard the front door open and close and someone quickly walking up the stairs. This was not normal. They didn't come in and say "Hello" or otherwise identify themselves. My daughter and her husband dashed up the stairs and no one was found. The kids were peacefully still asleep.

On another occasion, my daughter, her husband and the owners were having a dinner party and talk ran rather late. It was almost midnight when a loud female voice shouted down the stairs; "Why don't you people go home!"

They looked at each other and started to laugh. This further irritated the woman at the top of the stairs, who repeated her call for them to leave.

Then she mumbled and grumbled for a few minutes until my daughter thought they'd better go before the ghostly presence got any more upset.

A House Guest - Plus

A year ago, I had a guest coming to stay overnight. She and myself were going to repaint my deck furniture in preparation for a party for the Folk Song Society of Greater Boston. The party also was to include a canoe and kayak paddle before dinner and the sing. To get as much time as possible in to do the painting, I invited her to stay overnight.

The night before my friend came, I went into the guest room to check on the bed to make sure it was ready for its guest. As I entered the room, a distinct white square about 5 ½ feet on each side appeared in front of me. It was not totally threatening, but had a cautioning feeling about it. It must have been my late wife who was concerned about this lady about to come and sleep in *my wife's* bed. The square persisted all the time I was in the room, but only towards the north side of the room.

I tried to touch the square a couple of times, but each time it would move away from me. I blinked my eyes trying to see if it was something in my head, but it was not. I spoke saying; "Do not worry Amanda (my wife's name), it is not a romantic affair". With that, the square disappeared.

1639 House in Weymouth

This presence occupies a very early house where all manner of goings on are present. The first is an example of how children can see things we cannot. We have found this to be true in some of our other inquires.

When a 4-year old grandson came to this house, he wandered upstairs and on calling him down, he asked if he could play with the children upstairs. The owner knew of no children in the house, so they went up with him and he pointed to what they saw as an empty corner in the master bedroom and asked if he could play with them. They saw nothing in the corner.

The owner's sister and her husband once saw two women in old-fashioned clothes in the side doorway. When they approached them, they seemed to evaporate in the air.

The owner says she often hears two women loudly whispering in the kitchen behind her for 1-2 minutes. She turns and sees nothing.

Another presence is a mean old cuss as he/she rings the doorbell 2 or 3 times a year. It also pounds heavily on the front door and wakes she and her husband in the middle of the night. No one is ever there.

Doors in the master bedroom and the nursery have lives of their own and cannot be controlled. In the master bedroom especially, lights go on all by themselves even after changing bulbs. There are doorslamming sounds.

On top of all this, there are voices heard in the basement and in the barn.

In 1639, there were no TVs, CDs, or DVDs. The presence needed to have something to do.

My Father

My father lay dying of what the doctor called "a broken heart" as my mother had died only six weeks earlier. The doctor surmised that my father missed her so much, he just let go. He already had had two strokes and was limited in his mobility. He took to his bed, and so that someone could care for him, we moved him to my sister's house in Cohasset. While my sister was at work, we had a nurse come in to look after him. After only a few days he was sinking fast.

One afternoon, the nurse caring for him came in the room to check on him, as he seemed to be slipping away a lot that day. He said to her; "I'd like to have you to meet my wife." He pointed with his hand to a corner of the room where the nurse saw nothing, but thought she should acknowledge his remark. So she said; "How do you do." She was taken aback by this exchange as my father now seemed very alert from his appearance earlier in the day. After what she thought was some small talk between my father and his unseen wife, my father said; "We're going along now." And he died.

Neal's Personal Experience

Gettysburg:

This story is not from Scituate, but from a place famous for its happenings. Gettysburg. As most of you know Gettysburg is the site of the most horrific three days in the entire Civil War. The main armies of Lee and Meade met here. At first, the Southerners drove the Yankees back and they took up positions on the hills outside of Gettysburg. Thousands and thousands of men of the grey and blue would give their lives in those three days. The entire area has been set aside as a national park and it is here Lincoln gave his famous address at the opening of the National Cemetery.

The area has numerous books about sightings of ghosts and there are at least four videos re-enacting some of these stories. A movie company preparing the movie "Gettysburg" wanted to shoot in a spot known as the "Bloody Angle".

They carefully planned their shoot and the actors also known as re-enactors were ready to go. They turned on the camera. Or so they thought, but it would not work. They fiddled and diddled for a while and got a new camera. Same thing: zilch; nothing.

Almost everyone there felt the intensity of "something" while working there and even veteran moviemakers were bothered by it. They had to move the location to a place more friendly to the cameras and the crew.

One of the videos tells of a man and his wife meeting who they assumed was a re-enactor (they are plentiful at all times of the year. They dress as either a "rebel" or a Yankee and tour the park).   Anyway, they described this man as a rebel and *talked* with him. They asked if they could take his picture; "Sure." he replied. The man posed with him and then he and his wife posed with him and a passer-by took the picture for them. They had their arms across his shoulders! When the film came back, *no* soldier was in the middle of the photo!!!

Now you get an idea of what a visit to Gettysburg can be like. I know I'm sensitive to these things and was fully prepared to see something or someone. I came as a tourist and to see friends who lived nearby.

The night before my encounter, I had dinner with my friends in a famous tavern on the edge of town. We ate in the cellar as this is a popular hangout and the food a little less pricey. I asked the waitress if she had had any unusual experiences. She didn't elaborate, but said she felt very uncomfortable if she stayed late.

After dinner we took one of the "ghost" walking tours of Gettysburg where they show you around to famous ghost sightings and give you some history about the battle. There's the famous story of the Southern soldier who was a sniper holed up in a building in town and said he could hit the door latch on a house 300 yards away. He did, and his bullet bounced off the latch, went through the door, and killed a young woman inside. We didn't see or feel anything out of the ordinary that night. Although, I did feel uncomfortable at one point and a photo at that spot was blurred.

The next day I went to the Visitor's Center and after looking at things for a while, come out to the parking lot to get a jacket as the air conditioning got me chilled.

I didn't look towards my car until I was about 50 feet away. I looked right at my car and a man was sitting in it! I stopped and carefully looked. I was sure I'd locked it and first thought someone was stealing the car. Then, I noticed this person was not moving. Due to being in Gettysburg, of course, I then thought it might be a paranormal sighting. To assure myself that I wasn't seeing a reflection from another vehicle, I walked back and forth observing the figure, but there was no change. I looked around the parking lot to see if anyone else was nearby. None were. My next move was to look closely at the figure.

He had on a hat similar to the ones worn by Civil War cavalry officers, beige in color. The jacket appeared to be blue. By this time, I felt I was seeing re-enactor person, as there were quite a few there that day. I had just seen a General Longstreet re-enactor so that idea came to mind. I wondered how he had somehow gotten into my car. Then again, was he a ghost? To satisfy my curiosity, I started towards my car again. When I got about 25 feet away, the figure faded away and was gone!

This person was as solid and real as a live person.

On returning to Scituate, I did some research and found that the Visitor Center Parking Lot during the battle of Gettysburg was where a reserve cavalry unit was located on the second day of the battle. This person was astride his horse and had his head blown off by an artillery shell.

Baptist Church, Newton, MA

I'm a member of a gospel choir and one of our concerts was a graduation ceremony for a choir member in this church. Our choir was seated to the right and behind the altar. In the center of the alter area are some of the large organ pipes surrounded by a waist high wood casing.

As the sermon was going on, I observed out of the corner of my eye a woman come in from behind me and was crouching down somewhat and holding onto the wood casing surrounding the organ pipes. She wore a dark brown skirt and a cream colored blouse. Her hair was salt and pepper gray and she appeared to be in her late sixties. I wondered if she was a cleaning lady who crept in to see what the occasion was as it was not a Sunday. As everyone near the alter was either in the choir or was in cap and gown, it did seem that she was very much out of place and if someone saw her they would wonder what she was doing there. I nudged the person next to me to look at her and as we turned to look straight at her, she faded away. The woman next to me was taken aback and was visibly shaken. She would not discuss it with me afterwards. She couldn't admit to herself that it actually happened, I guess.

Kathie's Prologue

The Others Among Us

G rowing up in an Irish Catholic family very much open to miracles and the improbable provided a nurturing environment for an imaginative as well as an open mind. My grandmother, a County Kerry girl, wove mystical visions of the banshees who cry and wail, warning of an imminent death. Dancing among her tales were the Little People, those mischievous and ageless creatures who seem to mock as well as entertain the more adventurous of us. Look for them under, in, or around a Fairy Tree, that lone tree in the middle of a field or meadow. Be wary of them for their wits are sharp and they like nothing better than to have a grand laugh that might be heard for miles at your expense. She told me too, of the guardian angel who sat on the stairs just outside of her mother's room at night and would glow there, smiling at her, as if protecting or waiting for her, I don't know which. But the angel was as real to us as life and never questioned.

Miracles, too, were expected. We prayed for them and knew instinctively our prayers would be answered, if not with a resounding, "Yes", then perhaps a softer, "Not right now." I must say that I still believe this and God has been merciful. We also prayed to saints, who are God's emissaries. St. Jude, patron saint of hopeless cases, was my personal favorite because he defied the label mere humans ascribed to him; nothing, indeed, was hopeless when St. Jude was consulted. He seemed to me to be the approachable and fatherly saint who was always there for us and always listened. Isn't that what all of us still want, someone to be there for us and to listen? I used to pray to St. Jude for a classmate who was persecuted in and out of school by other children and worse, by our teachers. His life was a living hell. I learned how not to teach at the hands of cruel teachers, who labeled, undermined, and reduced his self-esteem to rubble. St. Jude stepped in and adopted him as a fellow labeled man and though he said, "not yet," he stepped up to the plate because the former classmate is a well-adjusted and successful man today. Was it St. Jude or the classmate's ability to transcend a less than stellar childhood? I think perhaps a combination would be a fair concession.

My hat is off to both.

Auntie Helen is worthy of an entire chapter of her own; in fact, her mere presence demands it. Additionally, she'll come back to haunt me if I don't give her her due here. Trust me, no one wants this high spirited, wild and beautiful, rangy, 84 year-old red head haunting us, so: "Here's to you, Helen, with love!" Helen is little changed from her youth. She is my Godmother and spent a great deal of time with me growing up. She has three sons and a daughter and was married to the sweet and equally roguish Jack. Jack is with us only in spirit now, but the two of them were stand-up comics before the term was commonly used. They were the George and Gracie of our family. In Jack's absence, however, Helen could still put on a good show. She had two major phases in her life: leopard for the first half, purple for the last. Picture a wild woman emerging from her home décor of early leopard only to find the woman decked head to foot in leopard patterns, as well. She was delighted to show you her leopard bloomers; in fact, total strangers were treated to them. Today we must shift our vision of Helen to all shades of purple; this is not an easy thing to do because something inside expects leopard and reverts back to it. Eccentricities aside, or perhaps just a step back, Helen has fulfilled her life's mission of making people laugh and helping them feel good about themselves. She augments her gifts to all of us with bottomless batches of her famous chocolate chip cookies that emerge from her oven by the ton. But I digress. Helen had only one paranormal experience, but it went on for years and always when she was in the same place. It badly frightened her and this woman is not easily frightened.

Helen is the only girl in her family, with four brothers: my father and three others. She was the darling child of my great-grandmother and would often be invited to visit Grandmother Abbie in her brownstone on West Newton St. in Boston. The boys were not invited. Helen and Abbie adored one another and were each other's playmates. She remembers staying with her every school vacation and they slept together in the same bed up on the second floor. She remembers raucous tenants above them causing the ceiling to fall in on them while they slept. She recalls the old coal stove with a fresh pot of coffee always brewing. Unhappily, she recalls also the cockroaches that infested the house. Helen was sixteen when Abbie passed away; she dearly missed her soul-friend and didn't know how she could live without her. She soon found out. When her parents were away, Helen was in charge of her brothers and in this role, slept in her parents' bed in their house on Earl Street in Quincy. She awoke one night to see Abbie seated in a chair beside the bed, staring at her. She thought it to be a bad dream, so she covered her head and burrowed under the covers. Upon venturing forth from the covers, Abbie was still there. She didn't speak to Helen; didn't move; just stared at her. This was the only room in the house Abbie visited but she came back for subsequent visits for years. Helen has never understood why Abbie didn't try to speak to her or comfort her the way she had in life. Helen was terrified and told her parents, my grandparents, about the apparition. My grandmother told her to keep praying for her, pray long and hard; she needs extra prayers to make her way to Heaven. Poor Abbie must have needed a lot of prayers because the visits went on for many years. This was Helen's only foray into the realm of the paranormal, but it has stayed with her most of her life.

Miracles were not exclusive to the Irish side of the family. My mother's people were from Nova Scotia. Among them were my mother's nine brothers; she was the only girl. During WWII, all but one of my uncles was sent off to military service. The one remaining, *Uncle Lester,* had health problems, and remained at home to care for his mother and mine. He awoke one night from a deep sleep to the sight, sounds, and smell of fire consuming his room. In the midst of panic and confusion there was an explosion and then a vivid vision of his brother's, my Uncle Ralph's, face looking at him through the smoke. He leapt from his bed and ran to the other bedrooms to rescue my mother and grandmother only to find there was no fire, no explosion, and no smoke. One can only speculate as to his bewilderment and that of my mother and grandmother when this night was over. Two weeks later the telegram arrived telling of my Uncle Ralph's death on the beach at Normandy. One cannot term this experience a miracle, per se, but certainly it defies explanation and qualifies under the heading of Unexplained. Clairvoyance, a vision, second sight, call it what you want but Uncle Lester would tell you he saw his brother the day he died, 3000 miles away.

Uncle Lester's experiences were not limited to visions; he was also a dowser. For those not initiated to folks with this amazing talent, may I suggest you've lead a deprived existence. Uncle Let's tool of choice in dowsing, which is the talent for finding water with a divining rod, was a right angle bent piece of heavy gauge copper wire that he secreted in the trunk of his car. The Boy Scouts of Holbrook, MA where he lived, would invite him along on camping trips because Uncle Let could find water anywhere by walking about holding his divining rod by either end and waiting for the apex to drop abruptly to the ground, indicating there was water below. He was a folk hero for his legendary abilities. He had a second home near Bridgeton, Maine and I loved his story of the engineers who were trying to dig a well for the complex next to where he resided. Everywhere the engineers dug produced little to no water. Uncle Lester, on more than one occasion, suggested they bore down about 20 feet over to the side of their failed attempts. On more than one occasion, he was dismissed as an eccentric. Not known for lack of persistence, Uncle Lester pestered them once again. This time, more to shut him up than anything else, the engineers bored down where Lester directed. Bingo! Under his divining rod lay all the water the complex could use. Not being a gloating man, Lester simply thanked them for their time and walked away, leaving behind several dropped jaws and new believers. To those of us open to this kind of thing, the response was simply a good laugh and an, "Of course! The poor things should have listened in the first place."

Lester told me my grandfather was also a dowser and was a seer, that is, he had visions of events that had not yet come to pass. They inevitably did, however, and this quiet, unassuming man was well known for being quite accurate when, indeed, he did speak of his visions, which was not often. When I consulted my mother about this years ago, she flatly rejected all of this as nonsense. She grew tight-lipped and might I suggest, frightened. She refused to comment on any of it and acted angry at the suggestion that any of this could be real. Shakespeare might have offered that she protested too much, leading me to wonder whether she may have had experiences of her own but was frightened by them. I can understand that better than many, because my experiences along these lines have also been frightening, but I am more open to them than my mother might have been. Ah well then, we all haven't been graced with life experiences and conditions that are conducive to open-mindedness. To some, open-mindedness is a choice which can be refused; to others a necessity.

In my own experience with second sight, there have been glimpses into the future and the past, and certain conditions have set the stage for the insight. I was either in a posttraumatic stress situation, was in a twilight semi-asleep/awake state, or was involved in an intense emotional friend or family relationship with those involved in the insight.

After my first son was born, I had postpartum depression. 14 hours of labor and an ensuing caesarian section left me weak and despondent for a very long time. It was during this period I awoke early one morning to a little girl standing beside my bed. I can still see her with her brunette curls ringing her delicate features on her face. She was about seven or eight years old and dressed in an old fashioned gown with a matching ornate bonnet. Her eyes were brown and she was pleading with me to help her. Her voice was so sad and sweet. I reached out to her and asked how I could help her. With this her body seemed to be drawn back into a vortex with her arms still reaching out to me. I called to her and asked her name. She called back to me, *"Maude Shaw,"* just before she was gone forever. She has not returned, though I remember the helplessness I felt at the time. I spoke to my mother that day of this incredible and equally disturbing dream. I asked her if she knew of anyone by that name, and indeed she did. I had a great aunt Maude Shaw, about whom she knew little. Was this a dream or was it the energy of an episode in Maude Shaw's life when she needed help and reached out through time to someone who was as helpless as she was at the time. I don't know, but I do know it was deeply disturbing and just the beginning of unexplained occurrences that accompany me to this day.

In actuality, my forays into the paranormal (a term I reluctantly use because my belief system includes them as very much part of the normal), have been few and far between. I'm most grateful for this because some of them have been quite alarming. Others of them have been of the "...of course..." variety. I consider them to be simply part of our lives, such as coincidences; perhaps meeting someone for the first time, yet knowing that somewhere, at some other place and time, I have known this person. Also, not knowing a loved one was coming to visit, but feeling it, and then having it happen; all of these I simply accept; be they heightened perception or something else, I don't know.

A concrete example of the "of course" variety is the day I left one of my work places on a Friday afternoon during which time I could be anywhere. At that time, Friday afternoons were work and duty free and I might meet a friend, visit a loved one in a nursing home, take care of business, but seldom was I home. This day was different. Something compelled me to hook a left out of the driveway of the workplace and drive directly home. As I turned one corner of my street, another car had just turned the other corner at the opposite end. Both cars met in the driveway simultaneously. The other car belonged to my son, *Chris*, who lived 60 miles away, who had been out of the state prior to this unplanned visit that propelled him toward Scituate, rather serendipitously with him not knowing my schedule or whereabouts. Earth shattering? Hardly, but my son and I share experiences like this habitually. His former wife was frightened by it on more than one occasion. On another unannounced visit I had an uncomfortable feeling that someone close was due to turn the corner of the road and went out on the back stairs to wait for whomever that might be. The same son of whom I just spoke, rounded the corner after another unplanned trip and said to her, "See, my Mum knew we were almost here." The poor thing started to shudder and found it difficult to speak for a while.

On that same visit, I was looking up the phone number of a friend in the Boston phone directory. As it was, my daughter-in-law was standing next to me when the book fell open to the very page I needed to locate that friend's name. I laughed and pointed out to her the coincidence, another "of course" scenario, but her eyes opened quite wide and she beat a hasty retreat for outside muttering something about not being able to handle this. I whispered a little "thank you for the assistance" and went about my business.

Away from the realm of the "of course" were the voices of *children* playing; voices I came to believe were unheard by anyone but me. My oldest sons were in elementary school at the time, but often when they were at school, I would hear soft muffled giggles and conversations carried on by very young children when my children were not here and neither was anyone else that I could see. The voices would emanate from the opposite floor or end of the house from where I was. I could never discern what the voices were saying but knew them to be the voices of children simply going about the business of being children. This was not alarming but certainly was disconcerting. Who could they be and why couldn't I see the source? As soon as I would investigate the source of the voices, they would cease or at least move to where I had just come. In time, I came to accept them and even welcome them. They were children after all, not posing any threat or mischief. In fact, I manufactured a little story about them that perhaps they were the spirits of some little ones lost to this life long ago, who enjoyed playing with my children and their toys and who maybe felt comfortable with me before moving on to where they rightfully should be. Not wishing to bear the brunt of skeptical glances and wishing to simply accept my little visitors, I seldom told anyone about these experiences, including my husband who was a pragmatist and would certainly, I thought, not understand.

One particular morning, all of that would change. It was very early and still dark, perhaps 5:00 AM and I was making lunches for my husband and children before breakfast when I became aware of a shadow peeking around the corner of the kitchen doorway. I thought it to be my second son who was similarly built and approximately the same age, about five. With my back to that doorway and working at a counter, my peripheral vision saw him clearly delineated and knew him to be a boy. He was teasing me, hiding when I turned around until I finally chased him upstairs, though I could not see him after he went around the corner. Thinking it was my second son, I ran to his room. Upon looking, there was absolutely no way that child had been awake and visiting me in the kitchen. He was out cold. So then I knew, there was another child in the house; this one was alone, and I was glad, again, that he chose me to whom he might show himself, if only peripherally. His appearance did, however, shake me up a bit and when my husband came down to breakfast, I was compelled to finally tell him of the children. Upon announcing that there were the ghosts of little children in the house, one of which I just saw, his face turned purple and he got a strange grin on his face. I thought, oh boy, here it comes, a barrage of skepticism. To my wonderment he exclaimed, "Thank God you've heard them, too!"

The ensuing outpouring of similar experiences was a shock for both of us. Here I thought I was the only one who had witnessed the voices when he was equally afraid of saying anything for fear of being thought of as less than mentally stable. He sometimes was able to come home a little earlier than the usual 8:00 and when he did, he liked to catch a nap before dinner. On days when the boys and I were out, he would inevitably hear the voices of the children from the bedroom and come downstairs to a room we used as a playroom to investigate. The results were always the same: the voices stopped upon his arrival, much the same way they did upon mine. I never feared to tell him of my experiences after that. In fact, the presence of the children discontinued after my third son was born. Sadly, they are no longer here and I miss them. Somehow it was comforting to know they were around.

I have spoken to two mediums, people who are sensitives and sense the presence of The Others. Each gave a different account as to who the children were. One said they were the miscarried babies of my Godfather and my aunt who sent them to me for safekeeping. The medium was from England and had never met me before and knew nothing of my circumstances. How did he know about those babies? He even knew they were miscarried and not aborted, announcing that in my family abortion would clearly be out of the question. He even went so far as to tell me where my Godfather had lived and worked and identifying his occupation.

Another medium told me they were the children of farmers who worked the Barker Farm years ago. The main structure of the now Barker Tavern is one of the oldest wooden structures in the country. It is only a few blocks from here and a stone wall still exists to demark the original boundary of the farm between its property and mine. This medium said the children died of influenza and said one of them is still here, though I've never sensed her. The others have all moved on. Whoever they were, they are gone now, as far as I know. Interestingly, I thought my two oldest sons were also skeptical until one day I was recounting some of this story and Chris countered with, "Do you really think that I haven't heard them, too? I have, for years only when I hear them, their voices are accompanied by the tinkling of bells or chimes." A song I wrote about our little friends now had a title: *"With the Tinkling of Bells, I hear their wee small voices…"*

How I wish I still could.

They were replaced it seems, for a while, by my father-in-law who passed away nine months before my third son was born. They never met one another but our family agreed that each would have enjoyed the other very much. They have much in common and my husband and I both saw Grandpa's gray eyes in our new son's. I believe he stayed around for about the next year and a half to make sure that the new arrival was ok. I was thinking of that wonderful scene from the Wizard of Oz of the wizard frantically trying to conceal his identity from the Lion, Tin Man, Straw Man, and Dorothy. He drew a drapery hastily around his concealed location and shouted into a microphone, "Pay no attention to that man behind the curtain!" I believe the man behind the curtain in my living room was Grandpa, who we desperately missed. He stuck around long enough to give his seal of approval to his new grandson with a few breaths and puffs on the curtain to let us know he was here and then moved on. He was a beautiful man and I think I know where he is now.

Subsequent to these visitors, we have had someone move furniture around in an upstairs bedroom when no one that we could see was upstairs. Casual, benign, simply going about his business is this unseen visitor who may even descend an area that used to be a staircase in the living room coming down directly from that bed room. Interestingly, it is that same room that managed to gather 37 bees one morning when there wasn't one single bee in the rest of the house. It was that room that once housed a family of mice. We had a big old lop-eared bunny who would beeline (pardon the pun) to that room when we let him loose and scamper into the closet to hide. It was also in that room that we once found a bat. On more than one occasion, various animals I've had in the house, stare at the exact same spot on the wall where the staircase descending from that room, used to be. Sometimes they simultaneously seem to see the same thing. I studied the same area and saw nothing, but then again animals are far more perceptive about these things than we are.

The medium seemed to think the unseen resident was a mentally challenged man who used to work on the fishing boats in the harbor and had a room in this house. He used to like to sit on the stairs, she said, and look out the window toward the harbor, exactly where the animals fix their stare. "What," one might ask, "is she talking about. That house isn't on the water." True enough; it no longer is, but it used to be right next to the Scituate Harbor Yacht club, indeed, on the water.

One other unusual happening in that room involved a resin eagle that was a gift to my son, Pat. It was heavy and stood about a foot high. It stood on the top shelf of a bookcase at the back of the bed in that room. Quite often we would hear a resounding bang upstairs in the middle of the floor of that same room and upon investigation, find the eagle had landed, face down. No one was in the room any of the times it took off and crash-landed. A dear friend and Irish mystic suggested moving the eagle to the desk rather than replacing it to the bed shelf. That was a good move because it hasn't budged since. Obviously, someone else liked the new arrangement much better than the old. Now that my youngest son uses that room, all of the activity has stopped. The youngest is a musician; maybe the visitor isn't fond of hard rock.

Two other random events come to mind when thinking of slightly off center occurrences in this house. One was immediately following my discharge from the hospital following hip surgery. It was just a couple days before Christmas and a dear friend,

friend, daughter to the aforementioned Irish mystic, was visiting for an evening to keep me company. A resounding double bang emanating from the dining room brought us both to attention. My friend knows the stories of this house and looked a bit frightened. No one else was at home and I couldn't move very well so she went to investigate and came back with two cast iron trivets, which were ordinarily standing on end on a plate rail along the upper wall of the dining room. They had not been moved in months, except for a light dusting done from floor level because of a persnickety hip. What induced them to propel themselves off of that rail and into the middle of the room to land on the floor befuddles me. I just thank heavens no one was passing by at that particular moment. It has never happened before or since and both trivets have been rooted in the same spot.

The other event involves an upstairs bookcase that is built into the wall in the corridor leading to my bedroom. One night my youngest son, Dan, and I were talking in the living room when we heard a crash upstairs. We joked that maybe that resin eagle had flown down to the other end of the house and nosedived into a wall or something similar. We didn't even bother to look at the time. However, when I went upstairs to go to bed I stumbled in the dark hallway just before stepping down off the threshold into my room. Upon turning on the light, I found my proverbial stumbling block: a pile of books had backed themselves off the shelf and landed directly below their shelf on the floor at the doorway. Don't ask me what propelled them off that shelf; I simply declared in my best authoritative mother/teacher voice, "That will be just about enough of that!" Maybe someone listened because it hasn't recurred. I only wish my students listened as well.

Martin

Martin deserves a chapter unto himself, and so allow me to introduce a gentleman sometimes referred to in his family as The Oracle. An impressive looking man of well over six feet with cornflower blue eyes that see right through you, a shock of white hair, a sharp wit, a wry sense of humor, an engaging brogue, and a healthy respect for, and acceptance of, mystical experience. Neither of us is at all sure that that's what it is, for it very well may be something we're simply not prepared to understand at this time but will in the future. However, I digress. Martin is the father of a dear friend who now lives here in Scituate but is from England. Martin was from Ireland originally, hailing from Ballybunion, County Kerry. He now lives in Reigate, in Surrey, England. At this writing he is 81 years old and going strong. I met him about 10 years ago after a couple of years of his daughter telling me, "You've got to meet my father." This is the same friend who witnessed the dispensing of the trivets from the plate rail.

Martin was a bit of a shock to me, upon meeting him. His son-in-law introduced him to me and Martin said nothing, simply approached me and took my face in his hands, visually studying my face. This was unnerving, having a total stranger look so intensely into my eyes before announcing, "So you're a Kerry girl," and indeed, that's where the Irish side of my family was from. How he knew that, I don't know. But then he's a man of many insights. By the way, he doesn't recall doing that. We've been fast friends and companions, though distant companions, ever since that day. He was one of those rare people who I'd just met but seem to have known from another time and place. Martin and I seem to have known each other forever. We could complete one another's sentences and often don't even have to speak to know what the other is thinking. We quiz one another about perceptions regarding certain people and events; rarely are we incongruous. There was an immediate meeting of the minds for Martin and me. We are fast friends to this day. But by now you know I'm setting the stage for something and that I am.

About three years into our friendship, I awoke in the early morning twilight time and sat bolt upright in my bed in a fit of anxiety. I could see a vision of an elongated brick building that appeared to be a hospital of some sort. It was night in the vision but many rooms in the three- story building were illuminated, as was the front of the building. Outside and in a driveway to the front of the building were ambulances with blue lights flashing. I did not see him, but I knew instinctively that Martin was in that building and in a

45

dire predicament, perhaps in great distress. The vision upset me so much I shook myself awake and got up. It was about 4:00 AM and I made a cup of coffee to try and calm my nerves.

My husband was still living and when he came downstairs for breakfast, I told him what I had seen. He no longer questioned these things, simply accepted them. He did tell me though, that if I ever had one of these about him, he didn't want to know about it. I couldn't blame him for that.

Mid-morning, with the vision still vivid and deeply troubling, I fired off a letter to Martin in England, begging him to make an appointment with his doctor to get his blood pressure checked. I told him I was worried about his health and that something wasn't right. I mailed the letter and felt a little better, hoping he'd heed my warning. This was a Tuesday. I spoke of none of this to Martin's daughter. On Saturday of that week I received a call from Martin's son-in-law, my friend's husband, telling me he had bad news for me. His wife had just flown to England to be with her father who had suffered a massive coronary while undergoing a stress test in the hospital. Martin actually died but was resuscitated. He was in the English hospital system's equivalent of the critical care unit in guarded condition.

My husband was standing beside me when I got this news and looked incredulous, exclaiming, "Oh, my God, you knew." At this point I went to pieces remembering the event of the prior Tuesday. My friend's husband then asked, "If M___ was here, would you visit her?" "Of course I would," was the obvious reply. He responded with, "Would you consider visiting me?" Knowing he was distraught over the condition of his father-in-law, a man he dearly loved, and 3000 miles removed from him, I was moved to visit and spend time with him and his children, Martin's grandchildren, who were also visibly shaken. My friend's husband is a scientist and a pragmatist; I did not tell him of my vision at first. I never thought he'd be open to anything like that, but after a lengthy discussion, I told him what I'd seen. He listened attentively the entire time and I braced myself for skepticism. It didn't come; in fact, he appeared flabbergasted. He told me he had worked in the hospital in which Martin was being treated and the building I described was exactly like it was, including the blue flashing lights on the ambulances, which I didn't know ambulances had in England.

My friend had arrived in England on Friday and found my letter waiting at her father's home when she got there. She was badly shaken after reading its contents, intending to read it to her father when he was conscious. I continued to worry about Martin and had a couple more experiences with him remotely. At one point I was standing at the foot of his hospital bed, yes, from 3000 miles away. He was sleeping and unaware of my presence. At one point my position shifted to the side of his bed where I held his hand, again unbeknownst to him. Eventually, when I could telephone Martin and speak to him, I told him of my vision. He told me he knew about it already; he had seen me. He also saw his mother who had passed away many years earlier. She was standing in the doorway of his room and he asked her if it was his time to go with her and she simply smiled and said, "No Martin, not yet. You have many more years to live." Martin eventually had quadruple bypass surgery, recovered, followed his doctor's orders, and willed himself back to good health where he remains today. I haven't seen him in over four years but we speak on the phone, write regularly, and sometimes meet halfway across the Atlantic on one wavelength or another.

Kathie's Sprites

So many of the stories we uncovered were fragments of conversations, little asides which were usually preceded by, "Did I ever tell you about the time when...."or "Yes, I had something like that happen to me, too. When I was a teenager....", etc. Each was a micro story unto itself. Each was fascinating and a window into a world about which we know very little.

In one of my writing classes I had a student, a man close to my age. He was an eager learner and had much to contribute to the class. He is also a veteran and active in the Student Veteran's Union. He is an affable man and already a fine writer and a great conversationalist. Over several years we have become friends. He is a no nonsense kind of guy and hardly the type of person I thought would be receptive to the subject of this book. I told him about it anyway and surprisingly, he had his own contribution. *John* is a recovered alcoholic and drug user who went through some very bad years, during which time he was estranged from his family. His mother loved John dearly and her heart ached for him as she thought he was lost from her and himself. Her wish and prayer was that her son take hold of his life and take it back. She passed away shortly before he did just that, but never knew that he had turned his life around and was soon to become the very straight, productive, and happy man he was always meant to be. One of John's greatest heartaches is that his mother didn't know about his turnaround; or does she. Interestingly, whenever John is deeply into one of his more introspective and inspired poems or articles of prose and finishes the piece, he looks down to see, not his handwriting, but that of his mother. He is totally unconscious of this as he is writing. Perhaps this is his mother's way of saying, "You've done good, my son. Let me help you now, as I couldn't before."

Another dear friend, who is a highly intelligent professional, told me that shortly after her mother passed away, she awoke in the middle of the night to find her standing beside her bed and smiling reassuringly at her. Grief? Need to see her Mum one more time? I don't know. Maybe Mum needed to see her one more time, as well. Dad needed to see her one last time before he rested, also, because he hitched a ride in the passenger seat of her car shortly after he passed away.

Not far away is *yet another friend* who tells me he has intense experiences of precognition, knowing events are going to happen before they actually do or knowing events are happening, when he has no access to information to support this intuition. He is as uncomfortable with these 'sessions' as I am. They usually involve situations about which we can do nothing but get upset, and that helps no one. In one such instance, he was playing football for his high school team that practiced about a mile and a half from his home. He suddenly became aware of smoke in the air and heard fire engines in the distance. Instantly he knew that his house was on fire and worse, his little brother was cowering under a bed to escape the flames. He bolted from the field and ran the harrowing trip home to have his worst fears confirmed. Firefighters had blocked off the area around his house and were trying desperately to fight the fire engulfing it. My friend knew what he had to do: he had to get to his little brother, after all, he knew exactly where he was. He tried to charge through the fire line but the firefighters held him back. He shouted to them that his brother was in there and pleaded with them to let him in, if they weren't going to try and save the boy. It was to no avail; the firefighters knew it was too dangerous for anyone to go in there. It was only after the flames subsided and some of the smoke had cleared that even worse fears were confirmed. His little brother did, indeed, die in the fire, exactly where my friend told the firefighters he would be. Another of his brothers would survive the fire and grow up to be a naval officer at the Pentagon on 9/11/2001 who would escape the direct hit by the marauding plane that crashed into it and exploded. Finding himself safe was not enough for him; perhaps inspired by memories of his lost little brother, he re-entered the burning building, not once, but six times to rescue great numbers of people.

Scituate's people have been very open and almost relieved to tell some of their stories to someone who wasn't judging them or listening to them with a steel-trap mind. One such person is a 75 year-old gentleman who is an *artist and photographer with a singing voice of an angel.* An intelligent and astute observer of the human condition, he is one of my favorite conversationalists. He told me of an experience he had during WWII when he was a 17 year-old new recruit. He was desperately lonely for home and family and was befriended by a kindly chaplain and priest who became a father substitute for this very unhappy boy. The two spent many happy hours together, exchanging notes on books, movies, world situations, and genuinely enjoying one another's company. The boy was the youngest of all of the recruits and chose not to go with the others this one particular evening when they were going bar hopping. He stayed back at the barracks and with his friend, the chaplain, gone overseas, he had little else to do but turn in to bed. Shortly after falling asleep, he awakened to a glowing light at the end of the barracks corridor. Within the light he could make out a figure of a man and could hear him calling his name. He recognized the voice of his dear friend, the chaplain, and was overjoyed but surprised to learn he was back from the war. The figure of the priest came a little closer but still remained distant as he spoke to him and said, "I have to go far away for awhile, my friend, but I wanted to say goodbye to you before I left. You will be all right and I will ask God to guide you and care for you. God bless you, my son." With this, the priest vanished as quickly as he arrived. My friend didn't think too much about it at the time, but a few weeks later he got the news that his friend, the chaplain, had been killed in battle overseas and never had returned to the States.

Who is *the little girl* with the long flaxen hair who waves from a porch on Scituate Ave. then disappears before your eyes? For that matter, who is the little girl peering from the window of the Lighthouse? More than a few have seen each.

What of the *apartment in the Harbor* that used to be a doctor's office, where a young woman awoke to find herself pinned to her bed, unable to move and nearly suffocated from the weight of an unseen body on top of her?

At least two houses on *Brook Street* have been reported as having residents who are not listed in the phone book or Street List of Residents. Most are benign, wispy, almost unseen folk going about their business, but when more than one real live person describes the same image, something's going on that's a little more than a curiosity. One house actually experienced what might be termed a poltergeist, that is a violent and chaotic energy surge, where household items are hurled across a room by unseen hands. As quickly as some of these events seem to invade a house, they also leave. I remember reading many years ago about a *former rectory* in Hanover where an unsuspecting priest, who lived there alone, would find objects moved, thrown, dropped. He pretty much dismissed these things, but when a torrent of water roared down a flight of stairs from an upstairs with no water source, he became alarmed and asked parishioners to take turns staying in the house with him from then on. They observed the same types of activity as did the priest. A new rectory was built and no further activity was noted, either in the new or old rectory.

A house near the tip of *Lighthouse Point* were so overwhelmed by unseen sources of activity, the residents sought spiritual guidance and asked that it be exorcised by a local clergyman.

An *antique tavern* and restaurant in Duxbury is well known for its minor disturbances such as candles on the tables that relight themselves after they've beet extinguished after hours. Closed and locked doors open of their own volition and glasses move off shelves. Rather tame and unthreatening until you retire briefly to the restroom upstairs and have an uncanny feeling someone is observing you. The police were summoned one early morning shortly after all had left the building. Alarms were going off and doors were wide open, though they had been secured before the management left. To the amazement of the police, the dark building was flooded with tiny white lights flashing like fireflies throughout the downstairs. The cash register was open and some money was floating in mid-air right over the till. None was stolen and no culprit was ever found, though more than one person was frightened silly by the rather unusual scene.

More than one local *library* has tales to tell. In an adjacent town, books have been observed backing themselves off shelves and falling on unsuspecting toes. The attic, however, appears to be well protected by a female presence that deeply resents her space being invaded. Just ask the unsuspecting electrician who tried to do some wiring up there and charged down the stairs shortly after arriving, shouting, "Get that one away from me!" It seems that a hysterical female figure flew at him and terrified the poor man. He did not return to finish the job. Rumor has it that the presence is a former librarian who regarded the library as her home. Apparently she still does. Another old library not far away boasts books that back themselves off shelves, sometimes just the ones you might be looking for!

An old home in the *Shore Acres* section of Scituate has its back to the road because it once had an unob-

structed view of the ocean from its vantage point to
the west of Hatherly Road. This is no longer the
case, with neighborhoods now surrounding what
had been the estate of a judge. Unfortunately, the
poor man took his life in the home. After his demise, the house was used as a rooming house and
space was rented out to transients and was often the
site of disturbances of the very human variety. A
neighbor recalled being a little girl and going with
her aunt who acted as a caretaker when the more re-
cent residents during the 30's and 40's were away.
Her aunt told her the place was haunted and they all
wondered who played the piano upstairs when the
residents were absent. According to another
neighbor, a blue iridescent light still glows in the attic window from time to time. Perhaps the judge
misses his piano and still looks for it or perhaps he's
hunting for the gravestone that for many years
leaned against the back of the house.

What of *the ancient tavern here in Scituate?* We've
spoken to several folks who have worked there and
each has a little different tale to tell. Who is the trans-
parent lady who resides on the upper-most floor?
Could she be the woman who was standing by a window of the garrison during colonial times, when a
bullet pierced it and her neck, taking her life? After
the linen on the tables has been changed for the last
time in an evening, from where comes the yellow
powder that settles on the clean cloths? Imagine being
the unsuspecting waitress who finally has a chance to

rest on a tall stool in the lounge at the end of a busy evening, only to have the stool rigorously spun back and forth by unseen hands, with her on it.

As Neal mentioned, the *Mann House* has its benign and unseen resident. I would have to question whether the resident is Percy Mann or perhaps a Native American. A visitor from Quincy photographed the outside of the Mann House and was most surprised when he developed his film. For there in front of the house was a Native American man with his arms folded on his chest, dressed as he would have been back in colonial times. After all, the original colonists did lay claim to the Native cornfields in that area when they arrived. The North River Road development was a farm when I first came to Scituate. In fact, it was a vegetable farm for the Native Americans, as well. Their burial grounds were there, but were torn asunder. At least two residents of North River Road have experienced chairs moving across the floor of their own volition. Perhaps the Native Americans are making a suggestion to us that they are still here.

In conclusion, my brother *Douglas* reminded me of the only paranormal experience he ever had. His was not in Scituate but in Quincy where we grew up and where he later had an apartment with his wife and two little daughters. Quite frankly, I was stunned when he told me this story because I didn't think he had room in his belief system for anything like this. However, as Neal has said, most of us are disbelievers until something like this happens to us, and it did happen to Douglas. It started with the antennae on the TV quivering to the point of dancing a jig; it then progressed to the refrigerator that started a slow jiggle right across the floor of the kitchen. My poor father was visiting one night when the refrigerator sashayed his way; needless to say, he was more than a little unnerved. My brother is a contractor; he immediately searched for a simple explanation: construction in the neighborhood, a jackhammer vibrating the street, etc. Simply stated: there is no explanation.

Jean

I magine yourself a teenage girl and waking from the depths of sleep to find a man leering at you from the end of your bed and who gradually fades away with your terrified screams. Now try and imagine telling your mother of this would-be nightmare only to have her confirm that she sees the same man hovering over her at night, as well. Jean and her mother were taunted and haunted by this nightly vision for years. Jean's brother Tom saw him as well, but only in passing in a hallway or at the other side of a room. To him the man was no bother; he'd simply greet him and continue on; no problem. But the women weren't too fond of him, especially when Jean awoke to find him pressing down on top of her. She actually had to push him off and yes, there was weight to this apparition. The family seems to think they knew the man in life; in fact, he was a tenant residing with his wife on the first floor of their two-family home in Hyde Park. The man's wife passed away there and shortly thereafter,

Jean's family asked him to move out to make room for another member of their family. He was none too happy with this and let his protest be known. Jean's family lost track of him after a while, only to have memory of him recharged with the reading of his obituary. It wasn't long after his demise that he started to pay regular house calls to Jean and her mother. They seemed to think that he was looking for his wife and not really them. How sad to wander through after-life, searching through the dusty corners of memory for vestiges of a lost love who had moved on. He did not follow them to their summer home in Scituate, however. There were others waiting to meet them there.

7th. Ave., Scituate, just up from Sand Hills beach, is bright, sunny, and pleasant, most of the time. But those of us who have been around awhile know how *The Avenues* are reclaimed by the ocean during every major ocean storm. Most of the homes have been raised and fortified now, but this was not the case before the Blizzard of '78; 7th and surrounding avenues are low ground where the high storm tides get land-locked and flood the homes behind the sea wall. Jean's family knew this from summering there for so many years, but after her father died, ironically he drowned, the family became year round residents of Scituate. The 7th. Ave. address had some surprises waiting for them. One took the form of a pirate with missing teeth, who would lean around corners and grin at different family members, always before a storm. Others were not so visible but would make their presences known by sweeping all ornamental pieces on the mantle onto the floor. At one point an ornamental glass lifted itself of an adjacent windowsill where mother was seated, and rolled across and around the floor to land at mother's feet.

The family had to be rescued from their home on the eve of the Blizzard of '78. The wind was furious and the waves were beginning to flow through the house. They had to get out for fear of losing their lives as well as their home. They were shuffled from the high school Red Cross temporary facility to family to friends and finally ended up staying at what was the Inn for All Seasons on Barker Road. These people were so good to them the whole time they were there, for which the family will be eternally grateful. They even allowed them to bring their dog, who had survived alone for 4 days in a neighboring house. The family wasn't long back in its home when disaster struck again the following winter.

Once again they had to leave their home, as did their neighbors. Once again, nature took its course and the house sustained rapacious wind and waves. After they recovered from this one, the decision was made to move. A flurry of unexpected activity began at this time. A picture over the mantle would fall off each time mention was made of moving. After Jean's brother bolted it to the chimney, it still came down. The glassware from the mantle was regularly wiped out when calls came in from realtors and prospective buyers. The family awoke to the shattering of glass they believed to be their French doors early one morning. They all heard it, all got up to investigate, and all found absolutely nothing broken. A woman guest who expressed disbelief in the stories presented to her re: the spirits in the house, had a coffee pot come flying across the dining room at her. Jean had a medium visit the house who seemed to think Jean's father was still there with them and that it was he who tried to warn them about the second storm. The poltergeist, the shake/rattle/and roller, seemed to be displeased with the prospect of them leaving. Jean told the new owners about the situation in the house, but they haven't experienced anything strange. This brings us to this concept to consider: do spirits follow people or houses? Sometimes both? Sometimes neither? Is it the ocean? The leigh lines (water tracts under houses) that attract lost souls? Jean offered me this thought: " Houses wait for their owners." She went on to talk of the "moving experience" of going to their next home, which ended up being in an old part of Plympton.

Many mishaps, false starts, fallen through agreements, and near-misses eventually drew Jean and her mother to Plympton to a 1690 cape with 2 Marriage Trees out front, English Ash trees named John and Priscilla. The ancient trees are majestic and protective of the quaint little home of white shingles that seems a little shy when one first approaches it. I wonder if it has taken on the demeanor of its other unseen inhabitants who are peeking out at me from the dark and passive windows.

The entrance room is elongated and sunlit; chock full of splendid little collected treasures: a teddy bear in an Irish sweater, glassware brought from Scituate of every color and hue, and antique furniture so complementary to the rest of the house. The feeling upon entering is one of warmth and delight; altogether welcoming. Every little nook and cranny has a new treasure begging to be discovered. I looked forward to stepping from this ante-room into the main house to the kitchen, where more treasures and artistic displays were beckoning to me. However, I did not expect the pressure change in the room, one step over the threshold. My ears immediately blocked and there was a pressure on my chest. I backed one step to the ante-room and it lifted. One step forward again and it returned. I spoke to Jean of the presence of women in the house. It seemed to me that women were the caretakers here; they were simultaneously nurturing and kind, guarded and strong, and wanted their presence known; almost like a warning to "Watch your step! We mean business!" We stayed in the antique kitchen for a long while as Jean told me of the phone calls made to the house when they first moved in, where someone would pick up the receiver and then place it down on a table without saying a word. She spoke of gifts, sometimes childlike but quite tangible: a child's bracelet with a tear drop pearl left by her mother's feet on the rug on Jean's birthday. I saw the bracelet and a pearl drop necklace that inexplicably appeared another time. Jean's brother saw a girl spinning in the corner of the great room. Jean has not seen her but her mother often saw people gathered around her bed; women. When I interviewed Tom, he told me of a workman who was laying down carpet in this house, thinking he was alone there working. He looked up to see a figure standing over him watching him work, with old-fashioned trousers and suspenders. In fact, the figure had his thumbs hooked in the suspenders. The figure vanished, but the workman's terror hasn't left him yet.

Jean did hear a gathering of men talking in the great room when she returned one day from church. The talk ceased as she approached to investigate; she then heard women chatting from an adjacent room, her bedroom; they, too, quieted down upon her approach. A troubling room for me and for Jean was the birthing room. Jean said it was an unhealthy room, that she felt sick in it and didn't spend much time in it. I felt pressure changes as I walked into it and felt there was a cloud in the room, though it was quite dry and the temperature was comfortable.

Mother's room was an energy center, according to Jean, as her mother oftentimes had visitors from another realm. The wood paneling over the fireplace in this room is in a Union Jack formation, but can also be construed as a witch's cross to keep away evil spirits. Certainly the only spirits Jean's mother ever encountered here were simple everyday people who were going about their simple everyday business. Jean had only one frightening encounter here and that was in her own room where she awoke one evening shortly after moving in. A man's hand was being pressed to her face; heel of the hand at her chin, bottom of the hand over her mouth, and fingers extended over her eyes. She jumped up in bed and pushed the hand away and after dismissing the idea of burglars, she determined this was a resident who was displeased with her company. She loudly announced, "Now look here! You will not frighten me from this house. You live here and so do I and if you ever lay hand on either me or my mother again, I will have you exorcised!" It never happened again, well, not to her. Did I tell you about the shady workmen?

Ah yes, well Jean was having some renovations done to the house and had hired some strangers who she suspected might be taking advantage of her and of her mother. There was a bad feeling around them and neither of them liked them. Obviously, the other residents of the house were not fond of them either. After a heated discussion in the kitchen, one of the workers grabbed his ears and yelled, "I'm getting out of here! There are ghosts in here and they don't like me. They're sharpening pencils in my ears!" I guess that'll do it every time! Remind me not to tick off these folks. They mean business!

How did the gold coin arrive on the mantle? Who repeatedly threw a cup mounted on the wall near the sink at any visiting children? Maybe according to the customs of another time period, they appeared rude or disrespectful; I don't pretend to understand these things. I just accept them as do Jean and her brother Tom, and as did her dear mother who passed away in the house several years ago. Although, I think she's still there taking care of Jean as she always did. To paraphrase an old adage about hell and fury, Heaven, too, has no blessing like a mother/daughter bond. Their love will sustain them through all stages of our existence. I wonder how many other mother/daughter units are coexisting with them. By the way, the only entity I could visualize was like a photographic negative of a 15-16 year old girl with straight dark hair, parted in the middle and pulled back close to her head. She was seated in mother's room by the window just gazing at mother's bed. She made no movement and did not seem to be aware of our presence. Quiz question: What color was the girl's hair as I saw her? If you guessed blonde, you are correct; it would be the opposite of what I saw in negative.

Jean's father was not a sensitive like the others in her family. For Jean, Tom, and her mother, however, this was a life-long condition. It was not learned or developed; it simply was. They were not and are not frightened by what they see and hear; they simply accept it and try to understand. Jean is most respectful of the unseen residents of her house. She says she is not the owner of the house. Whoever built it is the owner, but she's happy to share with all of the others and judging by the age of the house, well over 300 years, there are quite a few 'others'. I asked if I could take pictures inside the house but we decided together that perhaps this might be disrespectful to the other residents so I confined my picture taking to outside. I thank them all for allowing me to visit.

Kathie Lee

North Scituate

W e now move up to North Scituate to a corner home facing a major road. I was at a Scituate Historical Society meeting one evening when a woman approached me who I did not recognize. She was so kindly and dear; I knew I had met her before. Fortunately, she introduced herself and told me a story I was stunned to hear from her. She is a very devout religious woman whose husband, when he was with us, was also a prominent figure in his church. There is no way she could ever manufacture a story such as this one. I have since talked to a friend of their son who will also verify the following.

She told me of things that bang in the night and of the sound of something heavy rolling across the floor, though there was no evidence of a source of the sound or its end result. Doors slammed, walls produced a rapping sound, and footsteps were heard but their producers were unseen.

An unbidden visitor to her room affected her daughter the most. She would see a man standing and looking out the window. Her brother volunteered to sleep in the room to investigate the presence that terrified his sister. He awoke to see a solid figure of a bearded man with his hair slicked back who was gazing out the window but then turned and looked directly at him. It seems that some spirits can interact with us, though most of us pray they don't. Others are unaware of our presence and just go about their business as if we are not there, much as we do, I suppose.

The woman told me she asked a priest to come and help them, which he did. He did not exorcise the house, per se, but instead held a blessing ceremony involving a bowl of water and prayers that any evil presences would go away and for the rest to calm down. Even the dog was blessed. Their prayers were answered in the affirmative, for their presences ceased bothering them.

Kathie Lee

The Turret House

This house is a very busy house; maybe not for our eyes to see, but many unseen people are there. The first is a man who lived in a turret that once was attached to the house. It was a Victorian house and turrets were quite common on Victorian houses in those days.

We know it was a man because of his large physique and masculine attire. Though his face was never seen, the translucent figure dressed in an ankle length trench coat and broad-brimmed hat appeared to several of the boarders in this North Scituate house. All who experienced him made the same comments about him.

No one could enter the turret room without feeling a severe cold that seemed to penetrate to the bone. You could not breathe in this room as there was no air and the lungs would choke up and almost seize. This was not a comfortable place to hang out; at least not for those of us who are earthly.

The tenants quietly acknowledged his presence and had no choice but to respect his turret space. Each had seen him dart around a corner or appear in a hallway; a being that lived in the shadows, but bothered no one.

The owner of a company in Scituate Harbor reports a happening in her young life when she was a tenant in this boarding house. She attributes her rescue to the strange resident of the turret. She was a young mother with her first child. She was bringing the baby downstairs in her arms to show the newborn to her in-laws. It was an old house with an outside stairway. About halfway down, she caught her foot on one of the wooden planks. She felt herself falling forward, screamed, paniced, her mind racing, her life flashing before her. "I can't let go of my baby! What can I do to save her?" Her thoughts flew by in a millisecond.

Suddenly, an invisible force in the form of two unseen, cool hands pressed on her shoulders, slowing her fall and finally stopping her. They gently then guided her down the rest of the stairs. At the bottom, the cool presence vanished. She never saw the man in the long coat and broad-rimmed hat, but there is no doubt in her mind who was responsible for saving her and her baby that day. For her, he was a silent hero.

Who was this savior? We will never know. Yet, the house had one very helpful pair of hands. No other instance has ever occurred to her. It would seem odd that having had this one instance of an unnatural happening she would have had others, yet there are no others.

Later the turret was found to be leaking and the water was getting into the rest of the house; so it was decided to remove the turret. Everyone knew of the turret's resident and wondered what would become of him. They had only to wait for the final stages of renovation to discover that the man had not gone far. Directly below where the turret used to be was a room and the tenants found out they couldn't enter this room without the bone chilling cold and same gasping for air as they had when the turret was there. They wondered if he liked the new room as well as the turret.

Ah, but there's more.

On a church sponsored traveling supper many years ago, this house was the location for dessert. As we savored all the goodies offered, we heard footsteps across the floor upstairs. They were quite loud and all conversation stopped as people looked up towards the ceiling. The dog who was present in the room, sort of growled and his hair was standing straight up on his back. Then, there were distinct footsteps coming down the stairs a jingling noise, and an odd "tick" noise with each step. We looked out in the hall, saw no one pass by, but heard a loud slam as the front door closed.

The hostess apologized for the interruption and noted it was one of her ghosts. Seems the house was a rooming house during the Civil War.

To facilitate guests who had rooms upstairs, an outside stairway was built so their noise on entering the house wouldn't disturb those with rooms on the first floor. One of the roomers upstairs was a young lady. Her suitor, who lived next door, would come a'courtin'. He'd use the outside stairway to the upstairs parlor. Yet, for some reason he always went down the inside stairs when he left and slammed the door. Maybe she refused all of his advances each time he came.

Anyway, he went off to the Civil War as a cavalry officer and died in battle.

He returned to Scituate in lifeless form to continue his courtin'.

The jingling was his spurs and the odd "tick" noise we heard was his sword striking the edge of each stairway step.

My traveling group contained our minister Father Raymond Low of St. Luke's Episcopal Church in Scituate and he offered to exorcise the house if she wanted to make an appointment. He had recently exorcised a house on Cedar Point in Scituate. She was aghast and said: "Certainly not! This is a part of the house's history and a selling point if I ever choose to sell the house!"

J. Neal Gray

Surfside Road

The lady called into the Ilana Marks show the day after we taped a live broadcast on our topic and asked that I call her about her experiences.. The phone interview revealed a family situation that is blessed with love and special guidance from family members past and present.

Her Mum passed away but is still with her and her brother who has special needs, and for whom she has full care. Mum had only one leg and occasionally she hears the little crutch squeak. She passed papers on the Surfside Road home, the house her mother had dreamed of her whole life, on her mother's birthday, though Mum was now gone; or was she? On the lady's 49th birthday, she found a pink, heart-shaped rock wedged in the blue and white house. She thinks it was a birthday gift from Mum. She has a music box that both she and her mother loved that plays a song they enjoyed together, "Through the Years...". It keeps turning itself on.

She is like her mother, a deeply religious person. The rose figures deeply in Catholic beliefs as being the flower of the Blessed Virgin Mary. Her mother said the Rosary as part of her daily life and occasionally the smell of roses wafts by her, though no roses are present.

There may be other things going on in her house that is 90 years old. Faucets go on; the outdoor water spigot, which had been turned off for the winter, went on. Dishes have smashed and a window shade flew off the wall, which was no easy task because the shade attachments are depressed into a cradle holder in the window frame.

She has had other brushes with unexplained phenomena. When she was 29 years old, her very best friend, who was raised in her home by her mother, was murdered. The friend left behind two children. This woman's husband was not living with his family at the time because they were separated. When he took care of them after his wife's murder, he would sometimes find the baby rolled over who was too young to roll over by himself. Was mother still caring for baby? There was a crib for the baby downstairs in the father's home. The father would sometimes find a rocking chair moved over beside the crib and rocking, though no one was in the house to move the chair. Several people saw the shadowy figure of a woman sitting in the rocking chair. Father had trouble with this whole concept and eventually moved the chair out and gave it to her friend on Surfside Road. When she was caring for the baby, it seems that the shadowy figure moved with the chair and the baby, for she sees her, too.

Kathie Lee

Betty

The old wood frame duplex across from Paul Young's garage on First Parish Rd. had been around for a while. It had been burned by Prince Philip's warriors but somehow, still stood and had housed a good number of families, including my friend Betty's husband, two teenage daughters, and a preadolescent son. Betty was a sensitive; that is, she sometimes saw things happening before they happened, and often, experienced strange goings-on in the house.

I'd known Betty about a year when she told me of a disturbing dream she had in which her mother's face appeared and had a slash in the forehead and blood oozing from it. Betty was still so upset in the morning by the vision in her dream, she called her mother who was distraught. The prior evening, her mother heard her husband, who'd been drinking heavily and was known to be a mean drunk, coming into their apartment. In her haste to escape him, she didn't turn on a light in the dark and walked into a doorframe and had a nasty gash in her forehead.

Betty's daughters were students at the high school; they were lovely, gentle, and sweet tempered; interested in boys, jobs, school, and friends; in short, they were quite typical of their age group. Untypical, were their experiences in their second story bedroom. Time and time again they would awaken to see a large, burly, dark-haired man in a red shirt glaring at them while leaning over their bed. Their shrieks would bring both parents racing to their room only to find nothing at all. The girls, badly shaken, would beg to keep the light on. Moments later, the shrieks would begin again; it seems the man with the red shirt was not deterred by light and would return to appear menacingly above the bed. This happened infrequently but continued as long as they lived in the house.

Betty would often watch television late in the evening in her living room with the lights turned off and would sometimes drift off to sleep. She would sometimes awaken to see a translucent image of a matronly woman in a long dress and apron with a duster cap on her head. The image spoke not a word, simply moved from the kitchen, through the living room, and into the next room that was Betty's bedroom; this would sometimes occur in reverse order. Betty would sometimes sleep late in the morning but seldom past 8:00 because if she did, she'd awaken to someone or something slapping the bottoms of her feet. She felt that the ghostly lady of the house took exception to laggards and was urging her to get up and get going with her chores.

The ghostly lady was not the only spirit visitor to Betty's bedroom. She awoke one morning to see an old fashioned, accordion pleated camera, complete with black cape, zooming in on her. The image faded almost immediately, but Betty was quite rattled by the experience. Shortly after this event she was visiting an elderly neighbor from diagonally across First Parish Rd. During their chat, the neighbor asked Betty about her house. The neighbor wanted to know what the front room was used for now. She told him it was her bedroom. He could remember years ago when a former tenant in Betty's house lived there. But the former tenant didn't use the front room as a bedroom, he used it as a studio for his photography business. Needless to say, this lent nothing to poor Betty's piece of mind.

The only strange experience I had at this house was while visiting with my second son when he was about 3-4 years old. While Betty and I were sharing an early morning pot of coffee, Chris was in the living room watching Sesame Street. He was seated on the floor with the few small toys he brought with him. There was no one else in the house and no furniture near him. I could see him clearly from my seat in the kitchen. He jumped up from the floor and ran toward me, obviously alarmed by something and was rubbing his head. He told me someone had hit him on the back of his head. I assured him that no one else was in the house and that he'd probably backed into a coffee table, yet none was nearby. Soon he was appeased and resumed his seat on the floor in front of the television. Within five minutes, he bolted out of the living room and appeared to be airborne as he leaped into my lap and grasped his arms around my neck, terrified. He was crying so hard it took a while before I could make out his words that he'd been hit on the back of the head again by some unknown, unseen thing. We had to leave immediately and I could never get that child to enter Betty's house again.

Betty moved away shortly after my son's encounter with the unknown in that house and I've lost contact with her. I wonder if new restless spirits awaited her in her new home or if she and they are finally at peace.

Kathie Lee

Another Betty

B etty D. didn't always live in Scituate. She grew up in Boston behind the Faulkner Hospital. Her family bought this home but the former owner remained for a very long time; the family couldn't get her out. Soon after a threat of eviction, she passed away, well, at least she did in some respects. Footsteps were forever heard coming down the staircase of this center entrance colonial, though no one ever saw a maker of the footsteps. The family, in time, got used to this. A little harder to accept were the footsteps that came downstairs and headed outside, opening the front door and slamming it shut behind whoever it was. Once again, a human form was not present. Perhaps the human form was the vision of a woman Betty saw standing over her bed with arms extended over her head or the one who pleaded, "Help me," when Betty had a sweatshirt half off over her head one day. She also recollects the bed covers being lifted off the bed and dropped back down on her by unseen hands.

Betty moved to Scituate into a 13 room Victorian house that had once been moved and was used as a hospital at one time. It was a double house with a turret. Betty's room was directly below that of her daughters. At three in the morning she would awaken to hear furniture moving in her daughters' room. Upon investigation, no furniture had been moved but the moving sounds continued as long as she lived there. Betty's son took a room beside his sisters' room and often heard the moving furniture as well, but the girls never heard it.

Betty's son had his own encounter with the seeming unnatural. Pale and frightened, he emerged from the bathroom one day, wrapped in a towel, saying he had just seen a woman with long black hair and a floor length black dress walk into the room across from the bath. He followed her but there was no one there.

Odors figure prominently in Betty's experiences. This house had a strong odor of a pipe being smoked, though no one in the house smoked a pipe. In addition to pipe, other scents wafted by Betty's nose as soon as she laid her head on the pillow, distinct odors of pink cotton candy, stargazer lily, and a spicy exotic scent. Interestingly, when life circumstances forced Betty and her husband from this house, they sometimes found her at her new home. She called me to investigate the smell of lily; not just any lily, but stargazer lily just after she moved. I brought along my little beagle, Milo, to help with the investigation. I erroneously though that maybe a scent hound would be able to pick up on it, because I did not. Unfortunately, all he picked up on was Betty's bulldogs in the backyard. He was most interested in them.

Betty and I have become close friends and we share stories of our brief forays into the other world. She continues to be a strong, resilient, woman, despite or perhaps because of her sensitivities.

Betty introduced me to another friend who has her own stories and sensitivities, Fran.

Kathie Lee

Fran

F ran is also a sensitive and lives on a street with no fewer than three cemeteries. The hooded figures of an earlier story re-introduce themselves. Fran will see these monk-like entities drifting down the road in front of her house. They have no faces, only a dark space where a face would ordinarily be seen. These are not misguided spirits, as ghosts oftentimes appear to be. These have an aura of doom about them that is oppressive.

On this same street is an old and large home that was once a stage stop and used by the USO. It boasted 16 rooms and many acres. The house and property has been since split up and was empty for awhile except for one tenant, a young man who was rather anxious to tell her of something very unusual he had seen in the house. Drifting through the house was a gossamer girl in a white dress with a rose at the knee. She appeared to be looking for something and was quite distressed not to find it. The young man's sister saw her, too; so did a former owner. She has also been spotted in the barn door.

I must confess to packing my kids, a friend, and her kids into my car one late summer's night and driving over there to check out the house under the cover of darkness. Just as we drove up the drive of the house and could see its dark visage, a light came on in an attic window and the figure of a person gazed out at us. My little vintage Horizon never backed up so fast; unfortunately, I misjudged the curve of the driveway, backed over a bush, and ripped out my muffler, much to the delight of the kids who had their thrill and loved Mum's new hotrod.

Kathie Lee

Holly

The west side of Rt. 3A has many beautiful old homes with stories to tell. Holly's House is one of them, built in 1846 and once used as a hospital for sick children.

We visited this home at the invitation of Holly who kindly shared her stories with us. She is a dear young woman living there with her husband and young children. In fact, I was her son's first teacher. As the stories unfolded in this pristine antique, we learned that Holly had lost children before they were born. We also learned that the house had been in the same family for over 150 years. In many ways it still is, as we will learn.

The laughter of children is often heard here. After all, Holly's children are happy, sweet tempered, delightful children. As in my home, however, sometimes the sources of the soft voices and giggles are unseen and present when the children are not. A woman who was grandmother to the former family that lived here, spoke of hearing children's voices. Holly heard them, too. In fact, she and her husband awoke one night to a small voice crying, "Mommy, Mommy!" when no one else was awake. A contractor with whom we also spoke, told us of working outside on the house and hearing children playing inside when Holly had the kids elsewhere. He also spoke of having his tools disappear while he was working there and then to see them reappear in a different location. While working inside, he always felt that someone was leaning over his shoulder and watching him work. He also heard footsteps in the rooms above him as he worked, though no one was at home.

A young woman who helped Holly after the birth of her second child spoke of placing a rocking chair in the living room area near the television. When she left the room momentarily and returned, the rocking chair had been moved and was still rocking though no one else was in the house. Holly recalls leaving her newborn in a cradle in the living area adjacent to the kitchen, just long enough to check on the progress of dinner one evening. When she returned, the rocker had been moved next to the cradle and both were gently rocking. I had no such luck when my babies were coming along. How nice it would have been to have an extra set of hands to help out with them; though I think I would have been a little more unnerved than Holly was.

Maybe the unseen residents there enjoy modern technology because the TV would often turn itself on and off.

Sometimes the parallel universe could be a bit alarming. Holly recollects watching TV one evening and there was an enormous crash on the deck. She though perhaps a tree had fallen on it. Immediately following the crash a door slammed in the kitchen adjacent to the deck. Upon investigation, the door was closed and locked, there was no evidence of anything having crashed on or around her property, and the cellar door was latched.

The busiest time for most of these occurrences were, not surprisingly, when they first moved in and were doing a great deal of renovation. Holly's son was quite small when he spoke of something white hovering at the end of his bed that would disappear. It was at this time, also, when Holly was alone in the house and a marble rolled itself across the floor.

The former owner slept in an adjacent room to the living room. He died coming down the inside stairs. Could he still be walking up and down those stairs, for most visitors and residents of the house have fully expected to see someone at the top or bottom of those stairs after hearing the footsteps. However, no one appears. Perhaps it is the owner of the tiny antique women's boots or the larger man's boots that were found under the stairs that do the walking. Might it be him, also, who squirreled away over 100 packages of green Lucky Strike packs all crumpled up under the floorboards in the bathroom? Is he also the one who will slam an upstairs door shut right behind you as you leave that room? I checked this one out. The floorboards there are wide, the house is old, the door is sound and hung nicely. There is no wind source or slant to the doorframe that might force that door shut. However, I do not want to be mid-way through that door when someone decides it should be shut, as someone often does.

Holly's house is not the only house in the neighborhood with unseen residents. Diagonally across the road is a house that has a woman's presence strolling the upstairs corridor. The grandmother of that family died in the house. Perhaps she is still minding and keeping them in her own way. Rather comforting, in a way, well, in some cases, anyway.

Not all of Holly's unseen residents are comforting. About a year after our initial interview, I met Holly and her young son, who was about 4 at the time, down at The Harbor. I never solicit these stories from children; nor do I comment upon them. However, his mother asked him to tell me about the strange visitors to his room. He had known me a couple of years by then and was accustomed to talking to me about many topics, so the story poured forth. He spoke of seeing two disembodied heads floating mid-air over his bureau across from his bed while he was in it. These were heads of older women and were grotesque to him. They talked to each other in his presence and spoke about him, making fun of him in a mean-spirited way. He was quite frightened by them and quite graphic in speaking of them. I am perfectly cognizant of the fact that children have great imaginations and love to weave stories, most of which are fascinating. However, when a child speaks of such things with a hollow look of fear in his/her eyes, it behooves us, and them, to pay close attention. My heart ached for that little boy. I sincerely hope those two have found another place to vent their sinister nastiness.

The West End of Scituate boasts many houses like Holly's. May we introduce you to some others.

Kathie Lee

West End

Down the road from Martha's (next story) is an antique Cape with a curious history. I know of at least two realtors who would show the house when it came up for sale but they would not go inside, citing bone chilling cold and an oppressive eerie feeling that forced them outside.

At one time a husband, wife, and daughter lived happily in this home before something went very wrong. The daughter moved out and the husband was accused of murdering his wife. Her body was found in her car at the bottom of Accord Pond in nearby Hingham. The daughter, subsequently, tried to get back into the house to retrieve her things. Father wouldn't allow it so she broke in. Her father vowed he would shoot her if she ever came back.

A friend of mine lived there for a while with his wife, baby daughter, and his mother. He said he never noticed anything strange there, but his family did start to fall apart there. His mother's behavior was erratic and his wife left with his little girl. On his last day in the house he was sweeping out the kitchen after moving everything out. That's when he noticed the very large snake working its way across the kitchen floor. In all of his time there, he had never seen a snake before.

My cousin's daughter baby sits now and again for the current family. She hasn't noticed anything strange, either, but knows there is a presence of a woman in the barn on the property. She won't go in there for that reason. She prays the kids won't play hide and seek in there.

Kathie Lee

Martha

The West End of Scituate has a fascinating history with many stories to tell and many old houses in which to tell them. Martha lived in one of a pair of houses built for sisters by a loving father who simply reversed the floor plan, one from the other, and situated them next to one another near Mount Hope. The house in which Martha lived has been lovingly cared for and relatively devoid of visitors from another realm. However, Martha recalls being in her kitchen and glancing into the parlor, during one Christmas season. There seated on the sofa was a small white haired lady, an uninvited but welcome guest. Her hair was tied up in a knot at the back of her head. She was gazing at the Christmas tree. "Ok, Aunt Salome, I guess you approve of my being here," thought Martha. Aunt Salome was one of the sisters, long since gone, and the assumption was made that this image might be her. Upon investigating this hunch with a direct descendent, it appears her hunch was good because there in a picture the relative had was Aunt Salome herself, looking just as she did in Martha's parlor.

Another relative of Martha's had a more alarming experience of seeing a woman lying on the kitchen floor who appeared to be dead. The vision vanished, fortunately, and never reappeared.

Down the road from Martha's are many other antique homes with unusual histories and perhaps newer histories to come.

Kathie Lee

Cohasset Triangle

In houses up behind old soda shop (now a home) on Margin St., Cohasset, this area "felt" uncomfortable during my excursion up there several years ago and others said they felt the same way on that street. Could this be a small "bad zone" like the Bermuda Triangle, the Hobomock Swamp south of Brockton, or an area in Northern Connecticut.

Well, ahhh-haaa. A piece of history fits into this. Bob Fraser gives us some background on the history of the buildings on Cohasset Harbor. As he starts his story about what happened at Cohasset's Maritime Museum, I see some interesting things about the above "bad zone".

Cohasset Maritime Museum
by Robert Fraser as told to Neal Gray

The present Cohasset Maritime Museum was built, I believe, by Samuel Bates around 1754. He was taxed for a wharf in Cohasset Harbor that year. Although it was not the first wharf, it was the first stone wharf and is still in use today!

The building that is now the museum was his ship chandlery as he owned a fleet of fishing schooners. There was also a fish-packing shed on the wharf. Now long gone. The third building of his complex was a cooper's shop, that later became the Old Salt House [now a restaurant in the summer].

The salt came from salt works along the shore that became plentiful after the War of 1812. The salt was used to cure fish. Large fish flakes were placed on drying racks out on Bassing's Beach (probably a good place as there must have been a strong odor).

Samuel drowned in the fall of 1801, when his schooner, loaded with general cargo and headed for Boston, struck Brush Ledge. She sank with the loss of all aboard. The business was then bought from Samuel's widow by the Stockbridge brothers who, I believe, lived in the big double house at the corner of Margin [suspected "bad zone"] and Stockbridge at the Cove. Within a few years, they also met with a tragedy. One of the brothers and the other brother's wife and a couple of their kids, slipped off the Mill/Gulf River Bridge and drowned.

Then Jonathon Bates bought the business back into the Bates family. His brother was Martin Bates who was a fur importer in Boston. Martin sent his two sons, John and Charles, down to Cohasset to help out Jonathon. John Bates lived in the big hip-roofed house on North Main Street nearly opposite the Central Graveyard.

However, Charles didn't like the country and soon returned to Boston and his father's business. In later years, Charles came back and built a house near his brother's overlooking Little Harbor. The site today has a large hedge of Forsythia on it.

John died in 1886 at the age of 70. By then the fishing business was dead. Clarence Barron, Jessie, Jane and Hugh Bancroft's grandfather, bought the buildings to preserve the old flavor of the harbor. They were to be torn down around 1955 to widen the street (it never was) and Jessie gave the ship chandlery to the Cohasset Historical Society. The fish-packing shed was moved east on Border Street across from the yacht yard. At that time, Jessie's brother Hugh used it to store his boat in the winter. The chandlery was moved to the western end of Elm Street next to the Historic House in the village in two parts in 1957. The lower floor opened as a Maritime Museum in 1959. The second floor was opened in 1964.

What happened at the Museum:

In the fall of 1959, the society held its Annual Meeting in the Museum. The high spot was to be a talk by Francis Hagerty on the history of Cohasset's shipping. During his talk, we all heard someone walking around on the second floor, that then was storage. I, having found a seat on the stairs leading up to the second floor, was asked to go upstairs and tell whoever was there to stop making a noise. It was thought some kids had snuck in and were hiding upstairs. I looked around here and there, but could find no one. Although it was dark, there are bright streetlights on both sides of the building and the single upstairs room was quite bright. A short time later, footsteps were heard again, and again I looked around and didn't see anything. The third time really broke up the lecture, everyone was laughing (perhaps nervously). This time, I went all over everything and never found or saw a thing.

Every so often when one or another of us came in, we would hear someone walking around upstairs. It made no difference if it was dark or a bright sunny day. Eventually, we took it to be the ghost of John Bates who came back to see what happened to his building. As I was Custodian for the society, I often was there alone. A woman came one day when I was waiting for hostesses to come to the Historic House and the Independence Gown Museum [Neal's mother's wedding dress is there] as I had the keys to open those places. I had just started showing the woman around the Maritime Museum when one of the hostesses arrived. I excused myself and went to open the House. When I came back to the museum, the woman came up to me and in a low voice said; "There's someone upstairs." I assured her we were alone. She refused to go upstairs to see the rest of exhibits and I didn't press the point.

It got written up in the old Herald newspaper and that really brought out the "loonies" out of the woodwork. Since then I have downplayed any and all ghost stories that I have heard. It did interest ghost hunter Hans Holzer of New York City and he came here one night with Rex Trailer of WBZ-TV and a Mr. Silver of WGBH-TV who made it into a program for Channel 2, Boston's PBS station. Holzer later included it in his book "Ghosts of New England."

And it went on that way until about 1972 or so. David Wadsworth, (former curator/president of the society), told me Bates had come back a few years ago, but recently it had been quiet there.

Sincerely;

Bob (Robert Fraser) &
J. Neal Gray

Cohasset Triangle, Continued

At the end of Bob Fraser's story about the Maritime Museum there are these leads:

The double house on North Main Street, built by Capt. Adam Stowell in 1793, has the ghost of a peg-legged sailor in the attic stomping around. I'm not to sure who this is; it might be one of the Orcutts who lived here for years. Anyway, it is an old sea captain who had lost a leg at sea. When he came home, he would often upset his wife at one of her tea parties by showing up drunk. Finally, an outside staircase was built so he could go to his room in the attic without bothering anyone else in the house.

Another is on South Main Street (I think I got the right house here). It was built in 1755 by James Stoddard, and around 1900, Ezra Towle, a carpenter, lived here. Towle is believed to be the ghost here. About 30 years ago one of the owners told me of this and found his name board in the attic. They didn't go into too many details.

A little girl ghost has often been seen in the big gray house on Sohier Street just about opposite the Music Circus. Never heard any details of this though. Daniel [Lincoln] had this large grant of land from North Main along Sohier at least up to King Street (3A). He had a boat in Little Harbor by which he took produce to Boston. He was called "Daniel the boatman" and was a brother to Mordecai "the miller who lived on South Main near the Scituate line and his mill still stands on Mordecai Lincoln Road. The mill drew water from Hunter's Pond.

At rare intervals, someone is heard walking around the second floor of the present Art Center. The staff believes the footsteps are those of Margaret Dillon, (long time president of the society). I [Neal] myself, have heard the footsteps. I recently recalled the day. I was looking for the present director and was told she was upstairs. I heard the footsteps and thought, of course, it must be her. Yet, on arrival in the room, it was empty. Several of the staff have heard the footsteps as well.

There are other haunted houses I have heard about, but the details are very hazy. Like the house on Jerusalem Road that the owners claimed was set afire by ghosts some years ago.

Sincerely;

Bob Frazer &
J. Neal Gray

The Transient Ghost

On Buttonwood Lane in Scituate lives a ghost who moved with the family when they sold their old house in Cohasset. However, let's start at the beginning.

Pat lived in a house on Elm St. in Cohasset. When she first became aware of him, she noted that he was dressed as a Revolutionary soldier. She often saw him ambling around the house and he was no problem for her. Her very young children were able to converse with him. She named him Xerxes. His living quarters were in the cellar.

When she decided to sell that house and move to one in Scituate, the children asked her to bring Xerxes along. They thought he might be lonesome or not like the new owners. So on her last trip back to the old house, she went to the cellar stairs, and sat down on the top step. She explained to Xerxes (although at that moment she could not see him) what the children had said and would he like to come to the new house with her? She felt his coolness as she went to the car and had him get in the back of the station wagon. (I wonder what he thought of riding in an automobile? He was probably scared stiff)

At the new house, she opened the rear lid and asked him to follow her. This house had a Widow's Walk and she thought it would be much nicer than the cellar he had been living in. The kids were overjoyed that Xerxes had decided to come as they loved playing games with him. He seemed happy as well. Every time he was nearby the hair on the backs of the dog and cat would stand up straight and they would stare at him.

As the kids got older he wasn't seen as often and eventually, not at all. She forgot that he was still there. After a while the Widow's Walk on the roof was having problems with leaks and since no one used it, she asked a carpenter to remove it. The first night, the hole was covered by a tarp to protect against the weather. One of her children, now grown, was in the Air Force and away from home. During supper, all of a sudden, there was crashing and banging upstairs in what was her son's room. Rushing upstairs thinking the wind had blown the tarp off, she found her son's room in a shambles – closets emptied, drawers pulled out and dumped on the floor, everything overturned.

Then it hit her – in removing the Widow's Walk, she had destroyed Xerxes' living space. She sat down on the bed, the only thing he hadn't overturned and started to apologize to the unseen Xerxes. After quite a few minutes she felt that he accepted the loss and she sought to find him new quarters. There was a low attic off of one of the younger children's bedroom and that became his new home. Things again settled down and after a few weeks all was quiet around the house again.

When we came to interview her about having her story in our book, Xerxes made an unseen appearance because the dog growled and the hair on his back went straight up and he stared at our Revolutionary soldier once again.

Xerxes wanted to be in our book!

J. Neal Gray

Country Way

Country Way originally way called the Coast Road. It was the second road in the Plymouth Colonies. It naturally ran from Plymouth to Boston. Today it is called by many different names; East Street in Hingham, North and South Main Streets in Cohasset and Country Way here in Scituate. Many of our earliest houses are located on this road and several are the source of unexplained happenings.

In King Phillip's War, one house was used as a "safe" house for friendly (Christian) Indians wanting protection when a battle or skirmish came near. One such battle did occur at what is now the intersection of Route 3-A and Route 123 in Greenbush. The house in question was built around 1729 with some timbers having taken from another house built in 1700. When the battle in Greenbush took place this house was within a mile or so of the battle.

The present owner of the house has had several experiences with an unseen friendly ghost(s). One or more who are probably permanent residents in the house. One who was around during those fearful days of when King Phillip roamed the countryside.

She has had several ghost sightings and/or "feelings" as she calls them, to back up her belief that someone else shares this house with her and her family.

One past/present resident has been seen at least twice. In solid form; fully lifelike.

One night, when the children were young, she hired a young man to sit with the kids until she and her husband came home. When the returned, he was sitting at the kitchen table, hands clasped in prayer and apparently on the edge of panic. Nothing seemed out of order, but he was extremely anxious. He never would sit again – even at a higher hourly pay.

Ten years later, he told the owner what happened that night. I guess he felt by then he wouldn't be ridiculed or that he felt the memory would fade from him if he told the owner.

He said that when he was going from the kitchen to the family room to watch TV, he past by a small guest room on the first floor and saw a woman in Pilgrim garb rocking a baby in a cradle. Besides that, she was crying. Research by the present owner found that a woman who lived in the house lost her husband while he was at sea.

The babysitter took one look at this woman and rushed back into the kitchen. He was terrified! He never moved the rest of the time she and her husband were gone.

In 1994, her oldest son, then about 23 years old, walked into the family room and saw a woman holding a baby in her arms and standing in a corner. He had no knowledge of the babysitter's story. He couldn't believe his eyes. He kept this to himself, as he was worried that something was wrong with him. Finally, four years later, he related the story to his mother. At that time she shared the story of the babysitter with him and he was greatly relieved.

There is another story about this house and why it is called The Indian House. We will put it in our next book.

J. Neal Gray

Country Way, Again

When Neal and I were taping a live cable show on this topic with Ilana Marks, we had a call-in tell us he lived on Country Way and his daughter had taken classes with me. He was so enthusiastic that he came down to the studio to talk with us after the taping. His home on Country Way isn't that old but is on the site of a former apple orchard where a little girl used to play in the trees at the beginning of the century, according to one of his elderly neighbors. He and his wife have experienced the presence of a little girl; his wife has heard her talking in muffled tones to two other adult muffled voices in their attic. He has done one better than that; he's seen her. He will awaken to see her standing next to his bed, yet when he reaches out to her, she disappears. Their daughter often talks to someone in her closet and he wonders if it's an imaginary friend or his mysterious visitor. He has also awakened to see the head of a Charlie McCarthy-like doll with a red and white turtle neck sweater on the upper part of the doll. It floats in mid air. This vision is startling, whereas the vision of the child is not frightening at all. One of the studio technicians with us was a friend of his and had his own story to tell. He was house sitting for the family and had fallen asleep in front of the TV tuned to Channel 3 but when he awakened, it was on MTV.

Kathie Lee

Another Country Way

Most of us are old enough to remember the S.S.
Pierce Company, with its imports from all over
the world. Captain Pierce lived in Scituate in a couple of different locations. A long time friend of
mine lives in one. She resides in this house with her
children and a sometimes seen woman apparition.
She believes the woman to be Lucy Litchfield
Pierce in her wedding dress, which has a poof skirt,
and she wears a bonnet. She is very petite and has
made her appearance floating from the borning
room and out to the top of the captain's stairs. My
friend's father and girlfriend have also seen Lucy.
She manifests soon after a tragedy.

My friend is also a sensitive who picks up on feelings and sensations others may not. She recently had
major surgery and just before it she sensed the presence of her deceased husband. She could actually see
the gray flannel pants he always wore and she could

smell him. She said she could hear him, too, not with words exactly but through a kind of telepathy he assured her about her health.

She, like Holly, has a television that changes channels of its own volition. I guess even unseen cohabitants have disagreements over the remote control.

Kathie Lee

Country Way #4

Bob called me after seeing only the last few minutes of a rerun of a show we had taped with Ilana Marks on the topic of Spirited Scituate. He had his own experience while working in a Scituate home on the previous New Year's Eve day. He has a cleaning company and had just brought his equipment into the house on Country Way, just north of North Scituate Village. When he stood up there was a fog in front of him and a lovely fragrance; he had a distinct feeling that this presence was female, though he saw nothing but fog. This occurred at 11:00 AM and there was no one else in the home. He was not frightened by this, in fact, he had a peaceful feeling, as if someone thought enough of him to want herself made known to him.

Bob has had other experiences from time to time of this nature. During the '80's, he was working for a cable company in Cohasset and was doing some work on a house on Jerusalem Road. As he approached the tower area of this house, he saw a woman looking down at him from the tower. There was nothing strange about her, but he happened to mention the woman to someone who lived in the house. This person emphatically denied that Bob could see anyone in the tower. However, Bob insisted and the person who lived there finally showed him the tower room that had been boarded up and unused. Upon inquiry as to why the room was boarded up, the person told him that family members had had strange experiences in the tower; a woman had been pushed down the stairs by unseen hands and a knife was thrown. It would seem that "the lady" did not wish to be disturbed.

Bob has also awakened to see a little girl ¾ of the way up the wall of his bedroom; this was before he had children of his own, and though he was set back a bit by this presence, it did not alarm him. However, there were other presences that were far more disturbing; I'd go so far as to say terrifying.

When Bob was 18 years of age, he was sleeping in his bed and awoke to find himself pinned to his bed. He felt the weight of an unseen body that was preventing any movement. The figure of a man appeared at the foot of his bed. Bob said he was strikingly handsome. The man gestured Bob to move to the window and to look out into the yard of his house. He said his body seemed to fly out of itself toward the window. Upon looking out, he saw the man outside looking up at him, yet beside the man was Bob himself, digging in the ground. The man then said to him, "I just wanted you to see yourself digging your own grave." Badly frightened by this experience he was finally able to release himself from being pinned down and the man disappeared. Just telling me of this experience seemed to unnerve him. He said though this happened nearly 30 years ago, the memory is as vivid to him now as it was then.

"There's something else, and you're going to think I'm crazy," he added guardedly. I assured him that I thought nothing of the kind and that I had heard some pretty harrowing tales while researching this book. He proceeded when I asked him if he recognized the man in his dream; an uncle or a grandfather who passed on? He said no to those but added, "I know who it was! It was Satan." I then asked what he thought Satan would want of him and asked if he was a religious man. He answered, "I think Satan was jealous of me because I am a strong man with strong religious beliefs. I have researched several denominations of religions with my wife but have found none that has done it for me; yet I know what I believe." I also asked if he had had recurrences of this visit, to which he answered, "No. I just seem to have these things happen to me from time to time; usually they're not frightening at all, just strange." I also went so far as to ask him if he sought counseling after the Satanic experience. I know I would need it if this happened to me. He answered, "No; didn't think I needed it." Ladies and gentleman, I present to you a profile in courage.

Kathie Lee

The Most Haunted House

"St. Michael, the Archangel, protect us. St. Michael, the Archangel, protect us. Saint Michael, the Archangel, protect us. Jesus Christ protect this house." These prayers have woven a protective blanket with which this woman friend must cover herself to escape the evil presences in her home. From the first day her family moved to Scituate eleven years ago, there were reports of an apparition of an older lady standing at the bottom of the stairs facing the living room. This was observed by friends who baby-sat for the family's three small children and by the children themselves. Then there was the sound of glass breaking where there was no broken glass. Following closely was the laughing that would break out in a room where there was no one. The family sometimes would hear parties going on downstairs in their home, complete with voices, laughing, music; all of this goes on after the lights have been turned off and all have retired for the evening; well, not everyone, because when her husband, would investigate the uninvited guests, no one would be there, but every light in the downstairs would be on.

I met the family soon after they moved to Scituate from New Jersey. Their older daughter, who was about six years old at the time, was a student in an art class I taught. She and her younger brother and sister would sometimes accompany me when I was cantoring at church. What a joy it was to see three beautiful children, enjoying going to church as much as they do. They invited me home with them one Sunday where I was treated to their very special brand of hospitality at their gorgeous yet comfortable home on Meeting House Lane, in a little wooded hollow just below the Men of Kent Cemetery. The original house, which was situated on the same lot but not on the same foundation, burned to the ground in 1915. No one was at home at the time and arson was suspected. The current house was built shortly thereafter. This is a lovely home in an area that gives the illusion of being in a remote area, though it is in the middle of a neighborhood. Surrounded by stone walls which were erected by a former owner, Mrs. Bacon, and cushioned by lush shrubbery and trees with a hillside view of the marshlands and out to the ocean off second and third cliff, the house stands quiet and aloof with its antique aire and its many windows keeping watch on those without and within. The outside of the home recalls the days of the Irish Riviera, a name often attributed to the Minot area of Scituate that has become synonymous with Scituate proper, with its old fashioned opulence, plush porch, and many angled roof. However, much of the inside has been modernized to answer the needs of a family of the 1990's, complete with rope swings for the children attached to the beamed ceilings. In a culture where monotony of architecture tends to be the modern rule, this house offers a refreshing change, a unique and creative expression which begs for information about former owners.

Upon asking about former residents I was treated to the story of Mrs. Catherine Bacon who just happens to have been a close friend of Adolph Hitler. It seems that Hermann Wilhelm Goering, (yes, the very one) the head of the Luftwaffe and director of the Gestapo during WWII in Nazi Germany, needed a little vacation prior to the war, and Hitler was kind enough to send his friend to visit another friend in her lovely home by the sea in a far off place called Scituate, MA. While Goering was here he was so generous as to offer to teach Mrs. Bacon's German chauffeur how to swim. The gentleman gladly took him up on his offer. With this the two went down to the North River where Goering promptly threw the gentleman in the river where he began the long painful process of drowning. It was only when it appeared that the man had stopped struggling that Goering finally condescended to hauling him out; most likely, quite disdainfully. Nazi friends were not the only strange penchants of Mrs. Bacon.

Besides entertaining interesting guests, Mrs. Bacon enjoyed shooting, right out of her windows, at any non-human animal that walked. Bones were discovered under her porch, large bones; the bones of horses, cows, sheep, none of which she kept on her property.

Before Mrs. Bacon, an impressionist painter, Meteyard lived in the first house on the property (late 1800's-early 1900's) who used the house as a studio as well as a home and invited many artistic friends to visit, one of whom was Oscar Wilde. Just prior to the Meteyards, Mrs. Webb occupied the home and it appears, she still does, in one form or another. She enjoys standing at the foot of the stairs, observing the changes in her living room. I wonder if they lived with the things this family live with, not all of which are so pleasant.

Many of the happenings in the home seem strange, though benign. Lights will turn off and on at will; the heat will jack up and lower itself; light bulbs blow out a lot, at least two a week; doors open and close by themselves and sometimes lock themselves; often the door opening and closing will be preceded by a knocking upon it. If someone goes to answer the knocking there is often no one there; children's music will come out of nowhere; the piano sometimes plays itself, not a lot, but a little; music has started up on the entertainment system all by itself while company has been visiting; the water faucet in the kitchen sink turns itself on while the family is having dinner at the table directly in front of the sink; all of which is bizarre but hardly anything of which one would be terribly frightened. However, there are other things which are not so bland or tame; other things for which there is no explanation; other things which are positively terrifying.

Imagine yourself alone in this house in the middle of the day and hearing a loud repeated knock at the door only to answer the door and see no one except the people in the cars of the funeral procession which is passing your home on the way to the cemetery up the street. Imagine your shock as your favorite serving dish which you received as a wedding gift comes flying off a shelf and smashes into a million pieces on the floor. Imagine sitting with your spouse and hearing what sounds for all the world like a freight train coming directly at and through your house, blowing out a window, and continuing on its way. Imagine awakening to a house that is full of the smell of smoke, yet there is no fire and the smoke cannot be seen. Imagine raising dogs all of your life and wanting to share your love of animals with your children, yet three out of four dogs brought into the house start out as great little pets, and soon start to act strangely and then turn mean to the point where you have to find them other homes; and what if the fourth dog is starting to show similar characteristics, such as refusing to go into certain rooms, or barking at unseen objects or things, and over protectiveness. But most traumatizing of all are the small dark creatures who dwell in the darkness of the upstairs.

Several baby-sitters have seen the creatures and will not come back again. A brick mason was repairing a wall and a chimney upstairs in the house and after three days made his apologies and walked off the job; he said his religious beliefs would not suffer the goings on in that house. He also warned the woman that she should take precautions if she saw these creatures by three times begging the intercession of St. Michael the Archangel and then asking Jesus Christ to protect the house and its occupants; this was after three days of feeling something was watching him while he worked. It was a dreadful feeling that made him fear turning around to see whatever it was; however, when he chanced a look in a mirror, the thing was directly behind him and he saw it.

It was short and dark, about five feet in height, with no discernible face and appears hooded in darkness. More disturbing than the appearance is the feeling of impending doom that accompanies the appearance and the sense of foreboding and evil. In a small way, the woman was glad that another human being had seen the "grim reaper," as she terms "them," because she sees between three and six of these entities in her upstairs hallway quite often; always upstairs and always at night.

They appear menacing and block her passage from the bedroom to the bathroom. She has been traumatized more by them than by any other occurrence in her house. Initially a disbeliever, her husband has seen the creatures only once but his description matched hers. Each perceived the entities as having malevolent intent.

When Neal Gray and I visited with the family, the entire family was present, though the children were absent during discussions of "the grim reapers." However, the oldest daughter slipped into the room and sought the refuge of her Daddy's arms and did overhear some of the conversation. She then added,

"Oh, Mummy, I've seen one too! Remember when I saw that thing at the end of my brother's bed in his room when I was sleeping in there?"

"Oh, yes, I remember that, " replied her mother, to which I responded, not wishing to further frighten the girl,

"You know, I've talked to a lady recently who seems to see a motherly figure at the foot of her bed when she awakens in the middle of the night; perhaps what you see is your guardian angel!"

"No," she countered as she slowly moved her head from right to left and looked at me meaningfully.

"This isn't anything like that. It's short and it's dark and it's really scary. I couldn't see its face because it has a sort of hood over its head. I hid under the covers and didn't come out till morning."

So much for the children not seeing "the gnomes," as they call them. The children hear the knockings and the voices; they also see the lady at the bottom of the stairs. They were witness to the music coming on by itself and the tinkling of the piano keys. In fact, they had one of their own to tell me about.

"Mrs. Lee, come and see the footprint on the ceiling, " invited their daughter.

Upon entering a great room, the room where a neighbor told them, "they used to lay people out," where the rope swing is suspended from the beams, I was directed to look upward where there was, what appeared to be, a male shoe imprint with another starting behind it. Thinking that perhaps it was a roof leak, I questioned if they'd had leakage. The woman told me that the attic directly over this ceiling was bone dry and that no pipes ran over there. It will be interesting to see how the next spot develops.

I can usually pick up on children who are in need of help and I anticipated the possibility of a problem. My observations told me nothing of the kind; these kids are happy, upbeat, creative, bright, talented little kids whose parents adore them. In fact, the daughter felt the need to reassure me as she added,

"They've never hurt anyone. They're just here!"

The family has contacted specialists in dealing with the supernatural who have advised them to go to each corner of the house and say out loud,

"We know you are here; we're not afraid of you; we respect you; however, we do not want you in our home. Please leave."

Neal and I suggested they have the house exorcised; we know that both of our faiths understand that conditions do exist which cannot be explained and that prayers are answered. In the meantime, Neal has referred the family to a psychic with a very high success rate. Perhaps, these people will regain a sense of peace with the house and whatever also exists there.

Though neither Neal nor I experienced anything but warmth and hospitality while visiting this home, neither of us doubts the honesty or integrity of these people. We listened and we accept their story of their experience as given and we stand in awe of their bravery in staying where they are.

Kathie Lee

O'D's Irish Cottage

Meeting House Lane has offered several interesting stories, as one might expect of a street with no fewer than three cemeteries. One of the cemeteries is the oldest in town and a fascinating place to visit. The graves were disturbed when the road was widened. Could this be the source of the problem to one former resident who would observe cowl hooded monk-like short figures pacing the road in front of her home. Another family had a whole host of visitors in and out of the home who were uninvited and not what we would consider "of this world." The cowl hooded figures would line up in her upstairs hallway in the middle of the night; a profound deterrent to attending bathroom necessities when nature calls. I think I'd invest in a bedside porta-potty. But then, I digress. Another home I visited here is an antique bursting with personality and character; some of the characters I know first hand; others I've known about for some time but haven't seen.

My first visit to O'D's Irish Cottage had me standing outside for a few minutes, studying the gables and intriguing architecture of a time gone by. As I approached the rear door of the house, I had the distinct impression someone was smiling at me from the lawn swing, to my right. I sensed an older man sitting there with a broad pleasant demeanor. In fact, I nearly spoke to him but it quickly became apparent there was no one there. I could picture my hosts inside, looking out the kitchen window at me, curiously saying to themselves, "Who is she talking to? Did we invite a raving lunatic to our home?" The door to the kitchen then swung open, and my momentary lapse was soon adrift in the warmth of the loving family that resides therein. Aromatic cooking smells, Irish music wafting on a breeze, bright happy faces, a wee drop of the creature (well now, sometimes good conversation and spirited music needs a little oiling), and we were on our way through an afternoon and evening of pure delight. I'm a musician and so are my hosts, who are as passionate about their music as I am. It wasn't long before we unleashed the instruments, oiled our vocal chords once again, and got down to the serious business of Irish music. I can tell you, that having participated in several of these sessions, at their home and mine, there's nothing better for the soul. Sure, there's magic there!

It took me a while to bolster my courage to ask about the house and whether or not anything unexplained occurred there. Each responded the same way, with wide eyes and a questioning expression. "Why do you ask?" I finally broke down and told them of my experience upon approaching the house. Mrs. O'D clasped her hand over her mouth and whispered, "Oh my God; that was my father!" I quickly interjected, "No, you see, I just thought I saw a man there..." Mrs. O'D gently moved her head from side to side, assuring me that I did, indeed, see her father; the only problem was, he had passed away a few years before. "He loved that swing," she added, "and spent many happy hours there, greeting passersby. He would have loved you." Tears began to swell, in her eyes and mine, as she told me about him. I was moved that this delightful man of whom she spoke would grace me with a brief visit, if only on an altered level. Though I didn't actually speak to him before, now upon passing the swing, I always say, "Hi Dad! You're lookin' good today." There's no response, but I can't help but think he hears me and that old swing starts up a little, of its own volition. I think I would have loved him, too.

Dad on the swing opened the floodgate of stories about the house and former inhabitants, seen and unseen.

The O'D's have a large family that all lived in this house at one time or another. This family extended to both sets of parents. Mr. O'D's mother lived in a front room facing the street. Upon further investigation, I learned several elderly mothers of other families, also lived in that room at one time. Mum would often comment that there was a woman who would sit in the chair in the corner. She said the woman would occasionally walk across the room and then return to the chair. No one else ever saw this woman, but Mum swore she was there and that she would talk to her. "I'm English, " the woman confided to Mum. She was not frightened by her at all, in fact, she seemed comforted by her presence, ever watchful from the corner chair. When Mum was dying, she announced, "That woman isn't there anymore." When the funeral director visited the house upon Mum's passing, he offered, "I once picked up another woman from that same room. The woman died right in that chair in the corner. She was English."

One of the O'D's daughters had a boyfriend who saw a body lying on the floor; it soon faded, but gave him quite a fright. Though the daughter often heard unexplained sounds in the house, upstairs in particular, she never saw anything. But her boyfriend did. They were standing and facing one another, having a conversation upstairs, when the boyfriend quickly registered an astonished expression and pointed over her shoulder, saying, "There's a large man standing behind you in the corridor!" The daughter was badly frightened by this and told me, "I don't care about the unexplained noises and voices (yes, there are voices, too), but I don't want to see anything or have anything interact with me in any way! Just leave me alone and go about your business!" Interestingly, Mr. and Mrs. O'D are not aware of anything going on upstairs, however, there's much more to tell about downstairs.

Mrs. O'D and one of the daughters were downstairs watching TV in the middle rooms one evening. They both heard footsteps this one night, walk right across the floor, go to the middle of the room, and stop. When they told Mr. O'D about this upon his return, he laughed at them. He didn't laugh at them for long, however. Shortly thereafter, Mr. O'D moved the furniture in that room. Perhaps The Others didn't like this new arrangement because, when Mr. and Mrs. returned from a music gig one evening, and were seated in their new arrangement, the parade of footsteps marched right on into the room, as they did before, and stopped short, right in the middle of the room. Mr. O'D didn't laugh this time. He also tells of another time when they returned from a gig, and there in a small area between the sitting room and the parlor was a low-lying thick white fog. They both sensed a small child in the fog and this was profoundly disturbing to them.

Another time, when Mrs. O'D returned from her night shift as a nurse in a local residence for the elderly, she opened the door to the bathroom and was taken back by a low floating iridescent green light. She sensed a child in there, again, and was saddened for this poor lost soul. It hasn't recurred but she still half expects it to be floating there every time she opens that door.

Adjacent to the room with the English lady in the corner chair, is another sitting room. It is in this room that happy gatherings occur quite regularly and are heard by most members of the household; the only problem is, there's no one there when the door is opened. While the door is closed, however, many conversations are going on at once, always at a sub-auditory level, though. It sounds of chattering without any words being distinct. In this book there are several accounts of this phenomena. These are almost like tape recordings from another time period; no substance other than the sounds captured on a tape that is played somewhere in the ethos, over and over again. To wax lyrical here a moment, perhaps we, too, are reliving our lives on another level, as are they. Will imprints of our lives come back to future generations to replay themselves? Add to the parties in this room the smell of cigarette smoke, which returns with the conversations. Two family members smelled it last week; no one smokes in the house or out.

Mrs. O'D had two other experiences she shared with me. One involved her grandparents who used to help with the Thanksgiving dinner for their large family. The O'D's lived in the Humarock section of Scituate for a while and it was there that she felt the distinct presence of her long passed grandparents working along side her in the kitchen there. Grandfather would offer Grandmother a little glass of beer to salute the holiday. She felt him do it again and it warmed her heart to think they were still there with her. She dared not look about to see them directly; she was fearful of dispelling the magic of the moment.

Last, Mrs. O'D told me of the room at the nursing home that would occasionally glow with iridescence in the middle of the night. Residents would often complain of a man sitting in this room who wouldn't go away. "Make that man go away; I don't like him, " they'd complain, but the staff never saw anyone come or go. It was interesting to note the numbers of residents of that room who described the same man, the man the staff could never see. Mrs. O'D was only one of the people who spoke to me of this room. Other staff members have, as well.

The O'D's have created a haven for all family and visitors alike; why would residents from another time feel unwelcome there? After all, the Irish are renowned for their hospitality. Quite obviously, the non-Irish have found this out and refuse to leave. Do you blame them?

Kathie Lee

Epilogue

Waxing Lyrical

"That one is an Old Soul."

"She/he's been here before."

"He/she has crossed over to the other side."

Will we be coming back into this world until we get it right?

Have you ever felt a sense of instant recognition of a total stranger: "I've known that person before; where, how, and in what context?"

What brought this person into my life and why?

Have you ever felt you had a dream or conversation before, though both are long forgotten?

Are ghosts fragments of personalities of a person who has crossed over and the fragments remain in a former dwelling?

If life is present before birth and after death, are our spirits continuous? Are our bodies merely containers for our phase on earth? Is life in our bodies merely a transition? I was a child when I read Dr. Norman Vincent Peale's analysis of our lives. The relevance of his words have stayed with me all these years. He spoke of us in our mothers' wombs where every need was satisfied. We had all of the nutrients necessary for life. It was warm and comfortable there. We were protected and supported; somehow we perceived the love our parents had for us. Life was perfect there. It was what we knew. It was comfortable. Trouble loomed when sharp contractions squeezed in on us forcing us away from this Utopian existence. Sharp sounds now assaulted our ears; sensations of cold, and instability shook our worlds. Where did our womb go? Will we survive this horror of a new existence? Soon we find that arms and other bodies support us where the womb had been. Loving voices replace the steady beat and drone the heart provided. We are fed differently, but nonetheless, those needs are satisfied, as well. Once again we realize that most of the time, we are comfortable. At the other end of the spectrum, could it be that we fear the same instability, lack of support, and the unknown that we did before birth? It may also follow that death is but another transitive stage and that we will enter into a new world as we did once before, or many times before-depending on our belief systems. What then of the restless spirits, the ones that may still be with us long after death. Did they somehow miss the boat? Are they like photographic images left upon life here on earth? Are they remnants of energy which once comprised a person?

Some say these restless spirits have things they didn't finish in their mortal lives and have come back to get them done. Some feel that perhaps they've felt slighted in life and come back for revenge. As observed in the Gettysburg encounter, sometimes lives are ended abruptly, totally unexpectedly, and prematurely leaving unfinished lives. Some people experience cool spots or cold drafts when a spirit is passing where energy has been absorbed to assist in materializing. Do they know they are gone? Some interact with the human realm; others do not. Often reconstruction, remodeling, or rearranging a room or a house will bring about ghostly activity. It appears this is frowned upon in the other realm.

Seven years we've been investigating for this project and we are still asking the same questions, also the same questions that have been asked since human life began. We are no closer to understanding this alternate reality and probably are incapable, as human beings, of understanding it. We may only wonder and tell the stories to increase our awareness of another aspect of life, perhaps to be better able to appreciate this one.

In Retrospect

In the quiet and the stillness, I hear you,

Gentle souls that graced another time.

And now, too, elusive conversations tell me

That you are not gone, simply out of step,

Out of earshot, or is it me?

Though you're sometimes out of sight,

You are never out of time, for time is irrelevant.

Your shifting shade just out of range of my vision

Reminds me how transient this life is.

We are here for just a little while.

Only our memories of you,

and maybe yours of us, live on forever.

Kathie Mason Lee

Neal's Bio

N eal is a Renaissance Man. There isn't much he can't do or hasn't done, however he is not new to writing or photography. He is retired from his profession as Technical Writer and Publications Manager, though he still works in the maintenance field; not bad for an octogenarian. He is also a professional photographer whose artistry may be seen all over the South Shore, including Scituate, MA.

Neal is also heavily involved in music, singing in no fewer than four Gospel choirs: Joyful Voices of Inspiration, Boston Community Choir, New England Conservatory Millennium Gospel Choir, and the Boston Pops Gospel Choir. His voice also graces St. Luke's of Scituate choir, Scituate's Ceilidhe, and the Folk Song Society of Greater Boston.

Neal is a Navy Veteran of WWII and an honors graduate of the Vesper George School of Art.

Neal's wife, Amanda, passed away in 1994; he is left with the other love of his life: his daughter, Mimi, his son-in-law, and grandchildren. The word is also out that he has no fewer than 236 lady friends who he calls Angels. Need to know more? Ask him. There's no room here to get into that subject area which could be a book unto itself.

In regard to books, Neal is preparing two other books. One is on family history, beginning with the Count of Egmont in Flanders (Belgium and Holland) and the other on the history of his father's company, Gray & Davis, featuring his father's life.

Kathie's Bio

Kathie is a teacher of 36 years who currently teaches writing at the University of Massachusetts at Boston. She has written poetry, essays, articles, and prose, much of which has been published in magazines, journals, and newspapers. She also teaches music in educational programs all over the South Shore.

Kathie organized and created a setting for the perpetuity of oral tradition and music performance in Scituate through the Scituate Recreation Department, called Scituate's Ceilidhe (pron. kay-lee). In Ireland, a ceilidhe is a dance, however, this ceilidhe welcomes many forms of performance and participation. Kathie and Neal met at one of the first Scituate Ceilidhes back in 1994 and immediately began exchanging ghost stories. The rest is history.

Kathie's husband, Bob Lee, passed away in 1999; she is left with three of the best sons anyone could ever pray for: Pat, Chris, and Dan; she is also blessed with a daughter-in-law, Mary, and grandson: Robert Matthew Lee, one of the great lights of Kathie's life.

In addition to her teaching responsibilities, she is currently working on several stories for children and a music curriculum for pre-schoolers that will include audio and visual components.

Scituate, Massachusetts *is situated on the east coast, half way between Boston and Plymouth. Scituate is no longer the sleepy little fishing village, farming community, and summer vacation spot it once was, though each of these industries still thrives. Constant, however, is the siren song of its pristine beaches, the welcome of its salt water and equally salty air, the ancient beauty of the North River that once brought Native American people here to summer from their inland winter home, the quaint antiquity that beckons and charms, and the loyalty of its inhabitants, whether Townies or Newcomers. A rare secret is kept here; come and find us.*

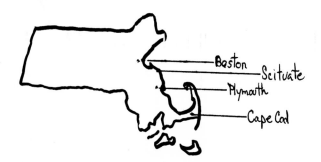